Practical Essays
on the Spirit's Fruit

Edited by Jennifer Maxey and Mark Mayberry

ISBN-10: 1-58427-531-6

ISBN-13: 978-1-58427-531-2

All graphics and photos: istockphoto.com. Front cover designed by Joanna Clem from istockphoto.com images.

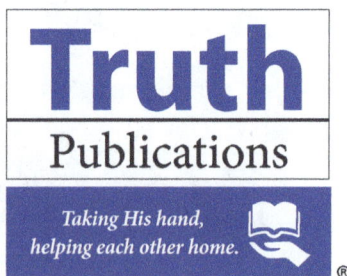

Truth
Publications

Taking His hand,
helping each other home.
®

Truth Publications, Inc.
CEI Bookstore
220 S. Marion St., Athens, AL 35611
855-492-6657
sales@truthpublications.com
www.truthbooks.com

Table of Contents

The Nature of Fruit
By Tracy Richardson

Introduction

Fruit is lovely, delightful, delectable, nourishing, enduring, and captivating. God instilled within fruit manifold attributes, which cause us to desire it. Its very nature beckons everyone to touch, taste, and see that it is good. The Greek word *karpos*, rendered "fruit," refers to "the product or outcome of something" *(BDAG, 509)*. Accordingly, love, joy, peace, patience, kindness, goodness, faithfulness, gentleness, and self-control is the singular desirable fruit that originates from God. It is the fruitful result of Christ's reign on the throne of our hearts. Cultivating this crop requires effort and exertion. As desirable as fruit may be, it requires us to strive, to strain, to stretch. Farming the vineyard of our hearts for this peaceable fruit requires arable ground, powerful seed, and yes, even adverse conditions. The pantry of the King is indeed stocked with that for which the world is starving. As kingdom citizens, we have been entrusted with sharing. Touching the lost, enlightening the deceived, and leading the blind can only happen when we ourselves are filled with His Spirit and bearing His fruit.

And do not be drunk with wine, in which is dissipation; but be filled with the Spirit (Eph. 5: 18).

But you are not in the flesh but in the Spirit, if indeed the Spirit of God dwells in you. Now if anyone does not have the Spirit of Christ, he is not His (Rom. 8:9).

. . . He who sows to the Spirit will of the Spirit reap everlasting life (Gal. 6:8).

Therefore, as we have opportunity, let us do good to all. . . (Gal. 6:10).

Earth's Unlikely Fruit

Arctic Cloudberries. Hidden cleverly away in the mountains of the Arctic is an extraordinary treasure. A wealth so cloistered and so coveted that native Norwegians refer to it as "gold of the Arctic." Once discovered, it is rarely sold. For a few short weeks in July, locals zealously don waterproof boots, gather foraging tools, and lug buckets into the muck of mosquito-infested marshes to mine their prize. It is the delectable cloudberry, a fruit that is valued not only for its rich, succulent taste and powerful healing properties but for the wild mystery of its unlikely birthplace.

City Strawberries. Equally incredible is how the freshest, sweetest, pesticide-free strawberries are now being raised in booming cities of France. Fertile with concrete and planted with skyscrapers, these cities are producing fruit 120 times better than traditional farms, without soil, year-round, and in converted shipping containers.

Ugandan Garden. Not so surprisingly, Uganda, Africa, with its reliable rainfall and rich soil, provides the perfect earthy environment for an overabundance of fruit crops. Winston Churchill observed on a trip there in 1908, "Uganda is from end to end one beautiful garden where the staple food of the people grows almost without labor. Does it not sound like a paradise on earth?" Doesn't it almost seem that fruit knows no limits? That she knows no partiality? Much like the sweet harvest that comes from God's Holy Spirit, her far-reaching goodness and faithfulness are universal, and "against such things, there is no law."

But the fruit of the Spirit is love, joy, peace, forbearance *(patience)*, kindness, goodness, faithfulness, gentleness, and self-control. Against such things there is no law *(Gal. 5:22-23)*.

Death's Unexpected Importance

Beneath the soil surface of a flourishing orchard exists an unseen world of fascinating activity. Perhaps one of the most chaotic, eccentric, and untidy materials on earth, dirt is a suitable environment for tiny seed. No ordinary dirt, though, will foster a healthy harvest. Luke 8:8 says, "Still other seed fell on good soil. It came up and yielded a crop, a hundred times more than was sown" *(NIV84)*. Only rich, velvety earth ready to receive the implanted germ can later boast a harvest. Only soil with access to oxygen, softened with water, and infused with nutrients will bring forth her peaceable fruit.

Then there's death. Healthy plants must have it. Amazingly, the lushest soil on the planet dubbed "black gold," and best known as humus, comprises about ten percent decomposition. Webster defines it as "a brown or black complex variable material resulting from the partial decomposition of plant or animal matter and forming the organic portion of soil."

While it escapes our notice, this kind of dirt is teeming with tiny organisms that work on lifeless leaves and animal flesh, changing decay into plant nourishment. Within the earth's soil, God exhibits death transformed into a fruitful life. And it's only within the good soil. Likewise, when the righteous seed of God's word is implanted, an abundant crop of His fruit springs forth from within receptive hearts. Are you daily dying to self, killing the old man of sinful passions, so that Christ may fill you up, living and acting, working, and reigning in the vineyard of your life?

I have been crucified with Christ. It is no longer I who live, but Christ who lives in me. . . (Gal. 2:20).

So then, brethren, we are under obligation, not to the flesh-for if you are living according to the flesh, you must die, but if by the Spirit you are putting to death the deeds of the body, you will live (Rom. 8:12-13).

Adversity's Undeniable Value

Your ordinary gardening guide will most likely never suggest the use of searing heat, frigid cold, or barren desert to grow your seeds. If it did, you'd quickly shelve it and reach for an easier plan. Adversity, though, brings its rewards. While fiery bush flames ravage the surrounding land, sturdy seed pods from the Banksias plant of Australia are being primed for achievement. These hardy wooden husks shut out the intense flames, later using harnessed heat to burst apart and share their contents. When living seeds and cleared land are united, life begins. Despite her stony plot and cold Arctic clime, the deserted Woolly Lousewort envelopes herself with purpose. Possessing woolen hairs, this petite edible plant embraces the sun's energy until she can produce striking purple flowers at winter's end.

Naturally, most of us prefer to *feel* the fruit of the Spirit. We don't prefer to work for it, especially if it involves adversity, suffering, or waiting. Like the Israelites, we also fail to appreciate the rugged terrain in which the Lord often plants us. Either we are crying for Canaan or whining for Egypt, but we never want the wilderness. Without better discernment, though, can we hope to grow? Oblivious to the future harvest, we stunt the Spirit's crop if we refuse to settle into the soil of trial. Nevertheless it is there that we find patience performing her perfect work. It is there we

find peace guarding our hearts and minds. It is there we find goodness sowing a crop of righteousness.

My brethren, count it all joy when you fall into divers temptations; Knowing this, that the trying of your faith, worketh patience. But let patience have her perfect work, that ye may be perfect and entire, wanting nothing (Jas. 1:2-4, KJV; emphasis mine).

And the peace of God, which surpasses all understanding, will guard your hearts and minds through Christ Jesus (Phil. 4:7).

And let us not grow weary while doing good, for in due season we shall reap if we do not lose heart (Eph. 6:9).

Seed's Inconceivable Power

An old Native American proverb says, "All the flowers of all the tomorrows are in the seeds of today." Within a solitary plant is the uncalculated capacity to produce countless more of itself. Therefore, it should not surprise us to learn that the primary purpose of plants is not to provide momentary food, temporary shade, or fleeting beauty. Instead, a plant's prime objective is to produce a lifetime of seeds. Seeds are imprinted with the unseen power to propagate the magnificent plant from which it came. As branches connected to the vine of Christ, we are endowed with this same profound power. Being blessed with the holy fruit of the Spirit, we daily scatter extraordinary seeds of righteousness along the ordinary paths of our lives into the hearts and minds of those around us. Even mundane tasks take on a heavenly hue when joined with the seed whose fruit is righteousness. Have you ever witnessed anger's face softening at the sound of your gentle answer? Have you lifted a harried heart by the kindness of your lips? Have you taken a quarrel by the hand and led it to peace? Have you ever invited self-control to join you on a shopping trip? Then you are cultivating the seeds of God today, which tomorrow will spring up into a harvest untold.

Sow for yourselves righteousness; real steadfast love. . . (Hos. 10:12, ESV).

I am the vine, and you are the branches. He who abides in Me, and I in him, bears much fruit; for without Me you can do nothing (John 15: 5, NKJV).

Take Off the Gloves

Diana, Princess of Wales, perhaps the most popular royal of all time, was best known for having the undaunted capacity for connecting with those who were the most unconnected in society. The leper, the AIDS patient, the impoverished; it didn't matter. Princess Di intimately met each one with kindness, joy, and gentleness. One particular person who knew her recalled after her death, "I ordered dozens and dozens of suede gloves in every shade for her because the royal family always wore gloves. Heaven knows where they all went because she never wore any of them. She wanted flesh to flesh contact."

Can this be said of you? Of me? Daughters of the King of kings, we of *all* people should lead the way in touching the lives and hearts of those around us. Beginning with our nearest neighbors, our family, and beyond,

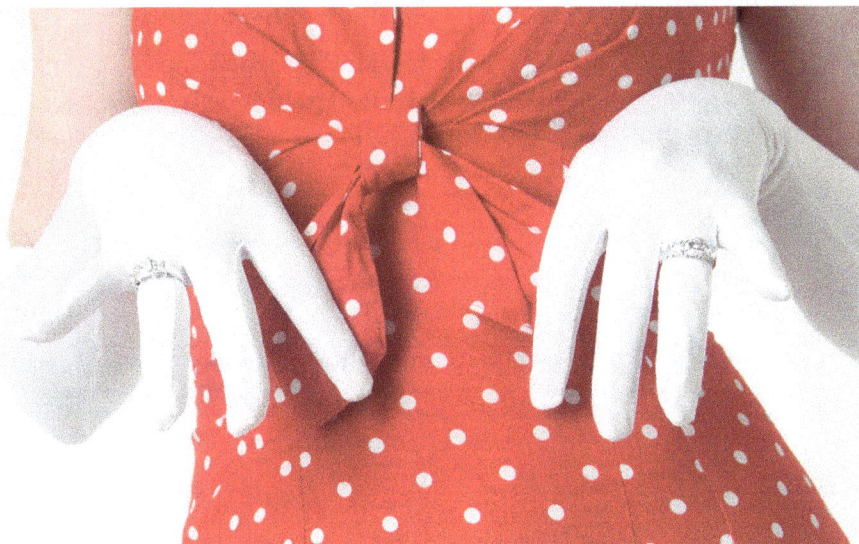

we should sow the holy seeds of God's Spirit bountifully. Fruit-bearing is something we cannot help *but* do if we are filling ourselves with God. Daily, dedicated Bible study and ceaseless praying soften the soil of our hearts, allowing Christ His rightful place there to reign. The prosperous seed of God's revealed thoughts must live within us, and we must die to ourselves. As our trials shape and mold us into the image of Christ, the result will be imperishable fruit that feeds us all and breaks no laws.

For the seed shall be prosperous, the vine shall give its fruit, the ground shall give her increase, and the heavens shall give their dew... *(Zech. 8:12)*.

Sources

BDAG = Arndt, William et al. *A Greek-English Lexicon of the New Testament and Other Early Christian Literature.* Chicago: University of Chicago Press, 2000.

"Humus." *Merriam-Webster's Collegiate Dictionary.* Springfield, MA: Merriam-Webster, 1996.

Thought Questions

1. How can love, joy, peace, patience, kindness, goodness, gentleness, faithfulness, and self-control all be understood as a single "fruit" instead of multiple "fruits" *(Gal. 6:22)*?

2. What does the phrase "against such there is no law" mean for you as a woman of faith *(Gal. 6:23)*?

3. Can you think of a time when you endured intense or prolonged adversity of heart, mind, or body? How did the experience change you? In what ways did it cause growth?

4. Who is someone in the Bible who endured intense or prolonged adversity? What was the result? Please provide Scripture references.

5. Throughout the day, how often do you think a woman of faith needs to reset or redirect her thoughts back to things above?

6. How can that redirection be accomplished?

7. Please provide two or three verses that address this issue.

8. As a woman of faith matures toward the image of Christ, when, where, and how might the Spirit's fruit emerge?

9. Can you think of an example from Scripture that depicts this fruit on display? Please provide Scripture reference.

Concept Seeds

To begin preparation for the next lesson, please consider the following question:

How much time this week have you spent with God in prayer, worship, or study of His word?

Jesus, the True Vine
By Kelly Cornwell

Introduction

I am the true vine, and My Father is the vinedresser. Every branch in Me that does not bear fruit, He takes away; and every branch that bears fruit, He prunes it so that it may bear more fruit. You are already clean because of the word which I have spoken to you. Abide in Me, and I in you. As the branch cannot bear fruit of itself unless it abides in the vine, so neither can you unless you abide in Me. I am the vine, you are the branches; he who abides in Me and I in him, he bears much fruit, for apart from Me you can do nothing. If anyone does not abide in Me, he is thrown away as a branch and dries up; and they gather them, and cast them into the fire and they are burned. If you abide in Me, and My words abide in you, ask whatever you wish, and it will be done for you. My Father is glorified by this, that you bear much fruit, and so prove to be My disciples. Just as the Father has loved Me, I have also loved you; abide in My love. If you keep My commandments, you will abide in My love; just as I have kept My Father's commandments and abide in His love. These things I have spoken to you so that My joy may be in you, and that your joy may be made full. This is My commandment, that you love one another, just as I have loved you (John 15:1-12, NASB).

Shortly before His death, Jesus presented the beautiful allegory of the True Vine is to His disciples. Jesus's illustration came in His farewell discourse to those who were closest to Him during His earthly life and served as an essential representation of the intimate union of believers with Jesus. Although the Lord was addressing His beloved disciples, how does the relationship He here specifies relate to our ability to bear fruit as Christian women? He tells us within this context. He is the vine, and we are the branches. The only way that we can bear fruit, the godly characteristics, and actions this study has focused upon, is through Him. "Abide in Me, and I in you. As the branch cannot bear fruit of itself, unless it abides in the vine, neither can you, unless you abide in Me" *(John 15:4)* We bear fruit by abiding in His words and abiding in His love, both of which leads us to abide in His presence.

Abide

Our purpose is to "abide in Him" and "bear much fruit." This is how we proclaim ourselves as His children. What does it mean to "abide"? The Greek word *menō* means to stay, abide, or remain. We stay close to the Vine, remaining close to the source of all of our spiritual nourishment. Jesus emphasizes the necessity to remain in union with Him with some urgency. In a physical vineyard, branches severed from the vine can not receive the nourishment needed to thrive and grow, but wither and die.

In His Words

Jesus stresses the sustenance found in His words. "If you abide in Me, and My words abide in you, you will ask what you desire, and it shall be done for you." Paul encourages the Christians at Colossae, "Let the word of God dwell in you richly" *(Col. 3:16)*. The idea expressed here is the concept of the Word dwelling within us to the point of an overflowing abundance. When we allow God's word to take up residence in our hearts, filling all the spaces of the inner man, it necessarily excludes all else. Intimately knowing His commandments and message of eternal life is how we continue close to Him. The study of God's word is the only path to sharing that promise with others.

It takes determination and perseverance to abide in His word. Discipline and forethought are required in our daily, mundane tasks. Do we prioritize as we busily strive to fulfill our various roles as women, seeking the Lord with our "whole heart"? In Psalm 119, the unnamed psalmist says, "Your

word I have hidden in my heart" *(v. 11)* and "Your servant meditates on Your statutes. Your testimonies also are my delight, and my counselors" *(v. 5)*. Are God's words ever before us? Do we meditate on Him when we are in the car, as we fold laundry, while we prepare dinner? It is easy to allow the monotony of the mundane to consume ourselves. I am guilty of allowing an entire day to pass without spending much or any time in His word. Jesus said, "If you love Me, you will keep my commandments." How can I know my Lord and abide in Him if I don't allow His word to live within me? Abiding in His words requires a faithful heart: "Your testimonies are wonderful; Therefore, my soul keeps them. The entrance of Your words gives light; It gives understanding to the simple. I opened my mouth and panted, For I longed for Your commandments" *(vv. 129-131)*. We should have a similar longing for His wisdom! Determined to remain and thrive as branches in the True Vine, may we strive to know Him through His words: "Now by this, we know that we know Him if we keep His commandments" *(1 John 2:3)*.

In His Love

Just as we strive to tarry close to Him through His word, we also seek to abide in His love. "As the Father loved me, I also have loved you; abide in My love. If you keep my commandments, you will abide in My love" *(John 15:9-10)*. Loving God naturally occurs when we appreciate the fact that He first loved us *(1 John 4:19)*. Although God's love is witnessed in many ways, the definitive demonstration of it was seen in His sending His Son to die for us *(1 John 3:16; 4:9)*. We appreciate the extraordinary nature of His love when we remember that we were once enemies, separated by our sins *(cf. Rom. 5:6-11)*.

Have you observed a vine with a solitary branch? Although we can never hope to emulate the depth of God's love, Jesus explains that we show our love for Him by obeying Him *(John 14:15ff)*. An aspect of this obedience is our willingness and determination to love one another. Love for one another manifests itself in many ways. As applicable to us as sisters in Christ, love can be expressed by offering encouragement, prayer,

guidance, support, and physical help. God blessed us with one another as we all work to bear fruit, the first of which is "love." The commandment we have from Him is that if we seek to love God, we must also love one another *(1 John 4:21)*. We abide in the True Vine, and He abides in us, when we practice the love of one another: "God is love, and he who abides in love abides in God, and God in him" *(1 John 4:16)*.

In His Presence

Isn't our goal to remain as close to our source of life as possible? Yet, how often do we seek to grow away from our roots? By keeping His commandments and demonstrating our love, we, the branches, abide in His presence. Often, *even* God's children may feel that a great distance must always exist between themselves and God. The question arises, "How can lowly men abide in His presence?" Jesus teaches us that there is a natural relationship between a true love of God and man's ability to abide in the Father and the Son and that Jesus has prepared a place for His people to be with Him *(John 14:1ff)*.

God did not send His Son to keep us at a distance; rather, Jesus enables us to draw near to Him because our sins being removed. We stay close by our desire to be in His presence. Our waking and constant prayers should be a sentiment similar to David's. "There is none upon earth that I desire besides you. . . . It is good for me to draw near to God" *(Ps. 73:25, 28)*. Jesus wants us to remain in His presence, close to the source of all we need to thrive and bear fruit.

Conclusion

It is impossible for us to bear fruit without the True Vine. If we don't abide in Him, Jesus teaches that we will be "cast out as a branch," "wither," and be "burned" *(John 15:7)*. How common is it for us to foolishly and pridefully believe that any fruit or godly characteristic that we embody somehow comes from our wisdom and understanding? Any love or peace or patience or self-control that we manifest arrives only as a direct result of belonging to and abiding in Christ, through His words and His love, and in His presence: "Abide in Me, and I in you. As the branch cannot bear fruit of itself, unless it abides in the vine, neither can you, unless you abide in Me" *(John 15:5)*.

Abiding is not meant to be a verb of inaction or passivity. We must actively fight to remain faithful. Paul uses words like "labor" and "striving" when he describes his walk with God *(Col. 1:29)*. It takes consistent effort to dwell in His word, continuously practice love, and seek a closer relationship with Him. Christ's parting words to His disciples apply to us as we work to produce fruit as branches on His vine. "By this, My Father is glorified, that you bear much fruit; so you will be My disciples." From a heart that desires God, we follow His commandments, living a life that glorifies God through our actions.

Thought Questions

1. How does Jesus's allegory of "I am the Vine; you are the branches" strengthen or affect your understanding about the church as the "body of Christ" *(Col. 1:18)*?

2. What is an attached branch's relationship to its vine?

3. What does the branch receive? What does the vine receive?

4. According to Jesus, what external evidence shows that a branch *(i.e., a Christian)* truly abides in the Vine *(i.e., Jesus)*?

5. Can you think of another New Testament passage that echoes or explains this concept?

6. Why would a woman who professes faith desire the presence of God in her life?

7. Why would a woman professing faith *not* desire the presence of God in her life?

8. How can a woman of faith know whether she is abiding in the Vine? Please find at least two other passages to support your answer.

Concept Seeds

To begin preparation for the next lesson, please consider the following question:

If a tree is "known by its fruit" *(Matt. 12:33)*, how does the fruit of my life identify me?

The Way We Know Them
By Sherelyn Mayberry

Introduction

How does one identify a plant? By looking at its fruit. Since each plant produces fruit after its own kind, thorn bushes will not yield figs, grapes, or thistles. Explaining this principle, Jesus said, "You will know them by their fruits" *(Matt. 7:15-20)*. Just as fruit reveals a plant's identity, the "fruits" of our lives manifest our heart's identity. We must receive the implanted seed, the word of God, which can save our souls *(Jas. 1:21)*. When this incorruptible seed is planted in receptive hearts, it brings forth believers who are "born again" in the likeness of Christ *(1 Pet. 1:23)*.

The Father's Vine

Jesus said, "I am the vine, you are the branches. He who abides in Me, and I in him, bears much fruit" *(John 15:5)*. The fruit of righteousness is a tree of life *(Prov. 11:30)*. When God's people, described by Isaiah as "the branch of My planting," bear the fruit of righteousness, the Lord is glorified *(Isa. 60:21)*.

How can we be fruitful? By letting the word of Christ dwell in our hearts. If I abide in the vine, living faithfully to the Lord, my branch will not be cast into the fire and burned, but I will be granted access to the tree of life for all eternity *(Rev. 22:14)*.

When the seed, the word of God, is planted in good and honest hearts, it grows and increases, yielding an abundant crop *(Mark 4:8)*. Allowing Scripture to discipline us produces "the peaceful fruit of righteousness"

(Heb. 12:11). Paul spoke of the "benefit" derived from being "freed from sin and enslaved to God," leading to sanctification and eternal life *(Rom. 6:22)*.

The Spirit's Fruit

Understanding that a tree bears fruit after its kind, we may ask, "From whence does the fruit of the Spirit originate *(Gal. 5:22)*?" The fruit is "of the Spirit." The Holy Spirit inspired the apostles in revealing the gospel of Christ *(John 16:13; Rom. 8:14; 1 Cor. 2:10-16)*. As we walk in the Spirit, Christ dwells in us, and we are rooted and grounded in love *(Eph. 3:16-17)*.

The Son's Nature

Because Jesus was "the Word" that became flesh *(John 1:14)*, His life actively portrayed God's will in a human body. His perfect and pure heart was seen in the things He did. Exemplifying the servant's heart, Jesus washed the disciples' feet *(John 13:15)*. He was patient with sinners, hoping that all would come to repentance and be saved *(1 Tim. 1:16)*. Our Lord learned obedience by the things which He suffered *(Heb. 5:8)*. In His life and death, Jesus Christ left an example for all to follow, so we might die to sin and live for righteousness *(1 Pet. 2:21-24)*. What a marvelous example of fruit-bearing!

The Christian's Treasure

Our "fruit" is compared to "treasure" that may be good or evil *(Luke 6:45)*. Our lives are shaped by what we value. Faithful Christians engage in good works and evidence proper attitudes. Personal application of God's word to our lives produces love, joy, and peace—the fruit of the Spirit. When nurtured and properly protected, such spiritual treasures will not fall into ruin or decay *(Matt. 6:19-20)*. However, those who practice the works of the flesh store up for themselves evil treasure *(hatred, murder, evil-speaking, etc.)* that leads to destruction.

Jesus said, "Where your treasure is, there your heart will be also" *(Matt. 6:21)*. The heart connects with the mind and intellect *(Prov. 23:7)*. Obedience, an act of the will, reflects a deliberate decision on our part *(Rom. 6:17)*. As the seat of emotions, the heart joins with our feelings and affections *(Isa. 65:14; Deut. 6:5)*. Moral values arise from the heart, reflecting a person's actual character *(1 Tim. 1:5)*. Finally, the heart is the place where God performs His work. When the seed is sown in good and honest hearts, it bears fruit with perseverance *(Matt. 13:19; Luke 8:15)*.

How Do These Truths Affect My Fruit-Bearing?

Relationship with God

Since God made us creatures of choice, I choose the object of my love *(Matt. 6:24)*. By setting my heart on this world, I become guilty of practicing the works of the flesh—the love of money *(1 Tim. 6:10)*, self *(2 Tim. 3:2)*, pleasure *(2 Tim. 3:4)*, and the praises of men *(John 12:42-43)*. However, if I set my heart on the kingdom of God, I bear the fruit of the Spirit, manifesting a genuine love for God *(Matt. 22:37-38)* and demonstrate such by keeping His commandments *(John 14:15; 1 John 2:3-5; 5:3)*.

Relationship with the Church

By bearing good fruit, I *(along with my brothers and sisters)* am built up, being knit together in love. United in Christ, we pattern our lives according to the treasures of wisdom and knowledge *(Col. 2:1-3; 1 Pet. 2:17)*. However, hating my brother evidences a lack of love for God, revealing my profession of love to be a lie *(1 John 4:7-8, 20-21)*.

Relationship with Our Family

In a family setting, the fruit of the Spirit gives birth to *agapē* love. Such love does not authorize the selfish pursuit of one's desires but involves emptying oneself—freely giving what the other needs. Husbands are commanded to love their wives *(Eph. 5:25-33)*. Wives respond with warm affection *(Titus 2:3-5)*. Children are also recipients of this sacrificial love. As a wife and mother bears good fruit, she is emotionally invested in the life of her family and sets the emotional tone of the home.

Relationship with Our Fellow Man

During this earthly sojourn, my fruit-bearing affects other temporal relationships. I am commanded to love my neighbor as myself *(Matt. 22:39; Luke 10-25-37)*. If I bear good fruit, I will treat others as I want to be treated. Love, for even one's enemies, is commanded *(Matt. 5:43-48)*. By doing good to those who hate me, praying for those who persecute me, I can successfully overcome evil with good *(Rom. 12:19-21)*.

Steps to Self-Check My Fruit-Bearing

I should examine self *(2 Cor. 13:5; Prov. 4:20-21)*. Am I honest with myself and my shortcomings?

I should treat others as I want to be treated *(Matt. 7:12; Luke 6:31)*. Am I living by the "Golden Rule?"

I should love my neighbor as myself *(Gal. 5:14)*. Am I concerned about the well-being of those around me?

I should humbly and reverently submit to God in obedience *(Prov. 22:4; Eccl. 12:13)*. Am I hiding God's word in my heart and keeping His commandments, or am I a disciple in name only?

I should feel ashamed when I sin against God *(2 Thess. 3:14; 2 Cor. 7:8-10)*. Am I tenderheartedly penitent or hard-heartedly rebellious?

I should not become puffed up or proud *(Luke 17:10; 2 Tim. 3:1-2; 1 Pet. 5:5)*. Do I have an over-inflated love of self, or do I exemplify the heart of a servant?

I should have a proper sense of self-worth in bearing fruit *(1 Cor. 6:20; 2 Thess. 1:11-12; 1 Pet. 4:11)*. Do I give God the glory in bearing fruit, or do I claim credit for myself?

"Yes, by your fruits the world is to know you, walking in love as children of day. Follow your guide, He passeth before you. Leading to realms of glorious day" *(Psalms, Hymns, and Spiritual Songs, #605)*. Bear precious fruit for Jesus today!!

Sources

Shaw, Knoles. "I Am the Vine." *Psalms, Hymns, and Spiritual Songs.*
   Sumphonia Productions, 2012.

Thought Questions

1. What does fruit reveal about its plant? What does fruit declare about its parent seed?

2. If Jesus is the Vine, and His people are the branches, to whom does the vineyard belong?

3. Please find at least two passages about vines or vineyards. What do you learn about your relationship with God from these verses?

4. In day to day living, what kinds of heart input interfere with the growth of God's seed within us?

5. Is there any way to avoid or minimize that kind of input?

6. Describe a challenging mother-child interaction that manifests the Spirit's fruit in the mother's heart.

7. Describe a challenging wife-husband interaction that manifests the Spirit's fruit in the wife's heart.

Concept Seeds

To begin preparation for the next lesson, please consider the following question:

How receptive is my heart to receive the guidance of God's word wherever it might lead me?

The Noble Soil
By Lindsay Wolfgang Mast

Introduction

Soil is a living ecosystem, and is a farmer's most precious asset. A farmer's productive capacity is directly related to the health of his or her soil—Howard Warren Buffett.

If you've ever set out to grow vegetables, fruits, or plants in your yard, you are well aware of this one thing: Gardening is tough. Farming is hard. Some of the most challenging, time-consuming, and expensive parts of the whole process pertain to preparing the soil for planting. There's land to clear and beds to build, nutrients to add, and pH balances to consider.

Why is it so hard to get started? Because the quality of the soil directly affects the quality of the plant that will grow from the soil. Jesus knew this. And even in our buy-everything-from-the-store society, we know this, too. As we contemplate the Christian walk and seek to cultivate the fruit of the Spirit, the parable of the sower teaches powerful and fundamental lessons.

The Seed Is the Word *(Luke 8:4-15)*

When we consider how to grow and produce spiritual fruit in our lives, we must understand what Jesus is saying in Luke 8, when He tells the story of the soils and then explains it further to His disciples. In verse 11, He explains the parable by first focusing upon the significance of the seed.

What is the seed? If the word of God is what must be planted to bear fruit of any kind, where must we turn to find this seed, obtain it, and then plant it? Obviously, we must preach the truth, following the New Testament as our pattern, and not turn aside to the right hand or the left.

Spiritual Nourishment to Produce Good Soil

In the conclusion of the parable, Jesus explains that the soil produces fruit when it is implanted in those with honest and good hearts. Such individuals are fruitful and enduring. Therefore, if we want to produce spiritual fruit and the fruit of the Spirit, there is work to be done on our part.

So, how do we nourish our hearts spiritually to cultivate good soil and thereby bear good and noble fruit? For one thing, we must put our trust entirely in God.

Look at Jeremiah 17:7-8. What does the Lord say about the person who trusts in Him? What human characteristics does that tree have? What will that tree produce?

Blessed is the man who trusts in the LORD and whose trust is the LORD. For he will be like a tree planted by the water, that extends its roots by a stream and will not fear when the heat comes; but its leaves will be green, and it will not be anxious in a year of drought nor cease to yield fruit (Jer. 17:7-8).

Now compare that to the person described in the verses just before that, Jeremiah 17:5-6. In what does that person trust? What is the outcome of that trust? How would you describe that person's life in terms of their ability to bear fruit?

Thus says the LORD, "Cursed is the man who trusts in mankind and makes flesh his strength, and whose heart turns away from the LORD. For he will be like a bush in the desert and will not see when prosperity comes, but will live in stony wastes in the wilderness, a land of salt without inhabitant" (Jer. 17:5-6).

Now think about what must be done to maintain that trust. Proverbs 4:23 says that we must guard our hearts above all else—more than our possessions or our marriage or our children or anything!

Finally, what happens if the soil of our hearts is not nourished and rich, ready to bear fruit? If we find rocks in our hearts or find our trust turning elsewhere, there is hope. Psalm 51:10 records a request David made of the Lord after one of the rockiest patches of his life. If things are not right in your life, take it to God in prayer. If your trust is lacking, and the soil of your heart is less-than-rich, ask for His help.

Impediments that Prevent Good Soil

If you read history about homesteading in Montana in the late 1800s, you will discover it was hard. Homesteaders had five years to "prove up" on their claims, and one of the major requirements was to farm the land. These driven people had to remove rocks from the ground and attempt to grow initial crops in sod. The grass in the sod would take nutrients from their corn, and the rock removal was backbreaking time-consuming work. For many, the dream of becoming an American landowner lived and often died based on how well they could prime and plant the land.

We know from Jesus's teaching that it's dangerous for us to have a heart that is "rocky" or "thorny." But just what does that mean for us on a day-to-day basis? What are the problems we can face that can keep the soil of our hearts from being ready to grow and produce fruit?

Rockiness

When soil is rocky, seeds have difficulty taking root and growing. Jesus likens this to those who gladly believe for a while but never develop sufficient root structure to withstand tests.

So, how do we develop roots that can stand up to the trials of life? First, we must understand that trials will come as we walk with Christ on this earth. Jesus himself assumed this and told us to expect it. What does Jesus say will happen in this world, in John 16:33?

Thankfully, when trials come, we can also look to Christ's example as way to overcome trials. Look at Matthew 4:1-11. Notice that Jesus responds in the same way to each of Satan's commands. How did He overcome each of Satan's attempts?

Jesus uses Scripture, the seed itself, to fight back against Satan. Knowing Scripture, knowing the seed, is paramount in defending ourselves from Satan's attacks. It is nearly impossible to be in the word too much—studying it, learning it, memorizing it—when it comes to defending ourselves from the evil one and from preparing our hearts to bear fruit.

Thorniness

This is a tough one. Why? Because these folks are true believers. Not newbie Christians, not people without genuine faith—these people believe; yet, they let the cares of this world choke out their faith. We see it all the time—and we have to guard against it by nourishing the soil of our hearts and keeping those thorns from taking root. What are the three basic categories of spiritual thorns that Jesus describes? See also Matthew 13:1-23 and Mark 4:1-20.

Worries about worldly things may include, the belief that wealth will make things better, or find expression in desire for things besides the Lord. All of these are real things that will keep us from producing fruit and from experiencing the fruit of the Spirit in our lives. So how do we live in this world yet guard against caring so much about worldly things that those cares choke out the word?

A vital part of the process is recognizing the thorns for what they are: cares about the things of this world over godly cares. What are two key heart traits that James warns us about in James 3:14-16?

Bitter envy and self-seeking can wreak havoc in our spiritual lives and in the lives of others around us. Philippians 2:3 adds to the idea of the devastation of selfish ambition by mentioning what trait?

The dangers of bitter envy, self-seeking *(some translations render this as "selfish ambition")*, and conceit require a constant check of our motives. As much as we might like to move through this world by habit, we must resist that tendency and ask ourselves, "Why do I want this?" and "What is my end game here?" and "Where is this desire coming from?"

In Matthew 6:19-21, Jesus tells us what our answer should be to these questions. Why do we do the things we do? The end game of our actions must be heaven-focused. Will getting our kids in the right school get them to heaven? Maybe, maybe not. Will getting the attention of that one man get us to heaven? Maybe, maybe not. Will running ourselves ragged in trying to serve in a way that doesn't suit our life or skills get us to heaven? Maybe, maybe not. The point is when we are fully confident that the choices we make will draw us *(and the people whose souls we are charged with stewarding)* closer to the Lord, the anxiety—the thorns—fade away.

How Does My Relationship with God Affect the Soil of My Heart?

If we are gardeners or farmers, we want a good crop each season. We invest time and energy, both physical and emotional. We want to see seeds take root, shoots come up through the ground, and ultimately a bountiful harvest that we can enjoy, share, or sell. Likewise, if we are Christians, we should all be striving to be the good soil Jesus talks about in Luke 8. We want that seed to take root in our hearts so we might bear fruit, know God, and make other disciples.

So, what happens if we find that there are rocks in our heart or that we have allowed thorns to take root and direct our actions in a way that is not God-centered? What if we look around and realize we are not bearing fruit or that the fruit we are bearing is sub-par or even rotten? How can we develop a heart that is like the good soil Jesus describes?

First, let's look at the characteristics of that heart. What characteristics does it possess? The heart that bears fruit is noble and good.

In the KJV, the word "noble," sometimes translated as "honest," comes from the Greek *kalos*. It means "beautiful, as an outward sign of the inward good, noble, honorable character; good, worthy, honorable, noble, and seen to be so" *(BibleHub.com)*.

This description focuses on actions we might perform that indicate our character. Someone with a noble heart has an honorable character, and that results in good, beautiful actions.

The word translated as "good" comes from the Greek *agathos* and means inherently *(intrinsically)* good, as to the believer. It describes what originates from God and is empowered by Him in their lives through faith.

That's important because it helps us to define what is good. Things that originate from God are good. A heart that will have fertile soil is one that desires, identifies, and emulates godliness—that is, true goodness.

How can we develop noble character and know what is good? The answer, again, is in knowing God better through Scripture. Look at Hebrews 4:11-12. In what three ways does the writer describe the word of God in verse 11? And what two things does it do?

Now ponder verse twelve. The good-soil heart is an honest one. How can the knowledge that God sees everything help us develop an honest heart? These verses offer an enormous challenge to us. The study of God's word will not be an easy one. When we open our Bible, we are opening a powerful tool that offers us a glimpse into our hearts—concerning which God already has complete knowledge. Seeing our hearts through the lens that God sees our hearts requires honesty and humility, and probably a fair amount of painful change. Yet, it's ground zero for getting out the thorns and the rocks and preparing to bear fruit.

2 Timothy 3 tells us again that Scripture will put us through a process that may not feel pleasant but will help us to bear fruit in our spiritual

life. Scripture is profitable for teaching, reproof, correction, and training in righteousness *(v. 16)*. Application of the truth to our lives leads to maturity *(v. 17)*.

How much reading do we need to do? Consider Joshua 1:8 and Nehemiah 8:3. While there are no set time limits, what are the common themes that occur in these verses, and more importantly, what is the outcome? In both cases, the dedication to the consistent study of Scripture led to greater knowledge and respect for God.

According to Romans 10:17, from where does faith come? Hearing the word of Christ! When our faith is weak, the Scriptures *(and only the Scriptures)* will build us back up!

Steps to Self-Check Whether My Heart Is Noble

Farmers and gardeners often test the soil in which they will be planting seeds to see if it's optimal for producing growth. As we seek to be like Christ, we should also check our hearts and make necessary adjustments so that we can bear fruit.

Based on what we know about the nature of Scripture, any reading of it will help us check our hearts. It's that powerful *(Heb. 4:12)*. Yet, just as a gardener wouldn't throw random chemicals just anywhere if she were trying to reach a specific pH soil balance, so likewise, there are specific things we can do to prepare our hearts to be fruitful.

Perhaps the simplest, most powerful self-check may be found in 1 Corinthians 13:4-8. Here we find the popular passage in which Paul describes the attributes of love. We know God is love *(1 John 4:7-11)*, and therefore we must have these attributes to be like Him. It is a truly powerful practice to reflect on this passage, putting our own name in the place of where it says "love" to see how we measure up. Try it:

_____ *suffers long and is kind.* _____ *does not envy;*

_____ *does not parade herself,* _____ *is not puffed up or*

arrogant; _____ *does not behave rudely,* _____ *does*

not seek its own, _____ *is not provoked,* _____ *thinks*

no evil (or keeps no account of evil); _____ *does not rejoice*

in iniquity, but _____ *rejoices in the truth; bears all things,*

_____ *believes all things,* _____ *hopes all*

things, _____ *endures all things.* _____ *never fails.*

Do you now have a better idea of areas in which you might need to check why you do what you do and try to better align your motives with those of God? The good news is, God wants us to be those things too and will be there to make the real change for us as we prayerfully try to be more like Him.

James 4:7-12 is another excellent place to go as we work on doing a self-check of the heart. His lofty list of requirements requires heart change every step of the way. Combined with constant prayer, though *(1 Thess. 5:17; Phil. 4:6-8)*, we can be confident that God will help us do all that He has asked of us.

Conclusion

If you've ever talked to growers at a local farmer's market, you can tell the deep relationship they have with what they have grown. They're proud of it because getting those plants from seed to harvest was hard work. The change—from rocky land to cultivated soil, to sprouts above the ground, to full, healthy onions or carrots or sunflowers or peonies, places a huge smile on their face. They offer visible results of change that produced fruit, and they have joy.

Likewise, God wants us to identify the challenges we may find in the soil of our hearts and then to help us remove any impediments to the growth of His word. By giving us Scripture and prayer, He has put a hoe, a weeder, and a spade in our hands and called us to use them. In doing His will in this, He, too, will feel the joy that comes from seeing heart soil go from rocky, thorny, and unusable to profitable, bearing fruit in all things. May God give the increase as we draw closer to Him and His ways.

Sources

HELPS Word-studies: "Kalos." *BibleHub.com.* https://www.biblehub.com/greek/2570.htm

Thought Questions:

1. In Luke 8:4-15, Jesus compares the quality of each kind of soil to various circumstances in life and qualities of the heart. What happens to those people who are like the soil in the path beside the field *(v. 12)*?

2. Describe some qualities of the people represented by the rocky soil, and note what happens to them *(v. 13)*.

3. The thorny soil *(v. 14)*?

4. The good ground *(v. 15)*?

5. Peter also equated the word of God to seed in 1 Peter 1:22-25. How does he describe the seed? How does he describe the word?

6. In James 4:7-12, what ten things are saints commanded to do? What is the result?

7. Discuss the warnings that Jesus offered about worry in Matthew 6:24-34.

Concept Seeds

To begin preparation for the next lesson, please consider the following questions:

How do I let love shine forth in my life? What are some things I do each day that show this?

Love
By Beth Stange

Introduction

But the fruit of the Spirit is love, joy, peace, patience, kindness, goodness, faithfulness, gentleness, self-control; against such things there is no law (Gal. 5:22-23, NASB).

But the fruit of the Spirit is love, joy, peace, longsuffering, kindness, goodness, faithfulness, gentleness, self-control. Against such there is no law (Gal. 5:22-23, NKJV).

As a young girl, one of my favorite religious songs was "This Little Light of Mine." It is a timeless gospel hymn with repetitive lyrics, making it an easy song for children to memorize. I can't say that I fully understood what the song meant as a small child, but I enjoyed singing it with enthusiasm! I felt joyful when I sang it, and I was excited to belt it out as loudly as I could. For those of us who sang this beloved Sunday School hymn as children, we look back on it with fondness. For others, however, this song carries a different and deeper meaning.

During the civil rights movement, many classic gospel songs became defining anthems of peace for those seeking equality. One such activist, Fannie Lou Hamer, had a special connection to "This Little Light of Mine." When Fannie got on a bus in 1962 to register to vote, she was rejected because she couldn't pass a literacy test. Later, on the ride home, her bus was pulled over, and the driver was arrested. As she waited to see how the situation would unfold, she began singing "This Little Light of Mine." This song had another meaning to her. How is it that one song can represent something so different to people from divergent walks of life?

Even though the context is different, perhaps there is a common thread that ties the meaning together. From an innocent child at church singing the lyrics with zeal to a brave woman on a bus singing from a place of uninhibited emotion, what binds these two together is *love*. Throughout the Bible, we are taught to let our light shine, "Let your light so shine before men, that they may see your good works and glorify your Father in heaven" *(Matt. 5:16)*. Letting our light shine is only possible with love in our hearts. If our daily walk is not filled with love for Jesus, love for others, and love for ourselves, we will never be able to "Let It Shine."

This little light of mine, I'm gonna let it shine.

This little light of mine, I'm gonna let it shine.

This little light of mine, I'm gonna let it shine.

Let it shine, let it shine, let it shine.

Definition

The Spirit's first fruit is *agapē*: "But the fruit of the Spirit is LOVE, joy, peace, longsuffering, kindness, goodness, faithfulness, gentleness, self-control. Against such there is no law" *(Gal. 5:22-23, emphasis mine)*.

God is *agapē*. First, this unconditional, sacrificial love defines God in His essential character *(1 John 4:8)*. The objectively self-existent One, God, in His essence, is synonymous with *agapē*. Love is also the medium—the channel, the way—in which Christians experience a relationship with God Himself. "God is love, and he who dwells in love dwells in God, and God in him" *(1 John 4:16)*.

Further, *agapē* clarifies what God demonstrates in the gift of His only Begotten Son. The *agapē* of God is the foundational motivation for His gift of Jesus *(John 3:16)*. The *agapē* of God is toward us, to the end that believers might experience life *(1 John 4:9)*. The *agapē* of God is abundantly sufficient to reach us, "while we were yet sinners" *(Rom. 5:8-9)*. *Agapē* determines what God yields in Christian lives as the Spirit's fruit *(Gal. 5:22)*. Because the actuality of God is *agapē*, it only makes sense that the seed of God, the word delivered by the Spirit, produces *agapē*. Thus, *agapē* transforms the self-willed sinner into the self-sacrificing servant. His seed produces after its own kind. God is *agapē*. God is love.

Active Love

This *agapē* love is more modernly referred to as "Christian love." We can define Christian love easily through the "Golden Rule," given by Jesus: "Therefore, whatever you want men to do to you, do also to them, for this is the Law and the Prophets" *(Matt. 7:12)*.

Growing up, I heard the rule quoted time and time again. . . at school, in church, and from my parents. "Treat others the way you want to be treated." What does that really mean? What if you do treat others the way you want to be treated, but they refuse to reciprocate?

First, realize that love is not necessarily a *feeling* for someone; rather, it is an *action*. You can feel "love" for someone through attraction or possibly even empathy toward a situation in their lives. The true meaning of love is expressed through our actions toward them. This is the love that Jesus speaks about in the parable of the good Samaritan *(Luke 10:30-37)*.

As Jesus recounts, "A certain man went down from Jerusalem to Jericho, and fell among thieves, who stripped him of his clothing, wounded him, and departed, leaving him half dead." Jesus then describes both the priest and the Levite who passed by this troubled man and took no action.

"But a certain Samaritan, as he journeyed, came where he was. And when he saw him, he had compassion. So he went to him and bandaged his wounds, pouring oil and wine; and he set him on his own animal, brought him to an inn, and took care of him." The good Samaritan felt empathy toward this man who needed help. He showed love toward his brother by taking action and caring for him. Jesus ends the parable by asking the question, "So which of these three do you think was neighbor to him who fell among the thieves?" Later telling the teacher of the law who had tested him to "Go and do likewise."

This *agapē*, or "brotherly love," is a perfect example of how we should let love be an action in our lives, not merely a feeling. Making strides to turn our Christian love into actions for others will keep Satan from blowing out our light for Jesus.

Won't let Satan blow it out.

I'm gonna let it shine.

Won't let Satan blow it out.

I'm gonna let it shine.

Let it shine, let it shine, let it shine.

Selfless Love

In Titus 3:2, Paul remarks on godly living by advising us to "Speak evil of no one, to be peaceable, gentle, showing all humility to all men."

What is interesting about this verse is that Paul doesn't say "showing humility to men." He says, "showing all humility to all men." Sometimes love is not about *us*. As Paul suggests, it's about being selfless enough to realize that we must love even when it is not convenient for us. Maybe someone has wronged us in the past, and we are having a tough time getting over the bitterness, hurt, and anger. Does this mean we give up on ever having a solid relationship with this person again? Of course not! This is why Paul says we are to "show all humility to all men." Living our lives through Jesus's example means that we are to put others before ourselves and show mercy and love to *all*, not just the people who are easy to love. He commanded His disciples, "Love your enemies, bless those who curse you, do good to those who hate you, and pray for those who spitefully use you and persecute you *(Matt. 5:44)*.

Today's selfish society makes this kind of love harder than ever to put into practice. Having a selfless love toward others is not easy when we are surrounded by a climate of instant gratification and divisiveness. However, we should take comfort in the example that Jesus set for us and know that it is possible. I can think of no purer love than taking ourselves out of the equation and merely doing things for others with no expectation of anything in return. There is no better way to "let our light shine" than for the love of Jesus to radiate through us and glorify Him.

Let it shine 'til Jesus comes.

I'm gonna let it shine.

Let it shine 'til Jesus comes.

I'm gonna let it shine.

Let it shine, let it shine, let it shine.

Relational Love

There are many relationships in this life that are founded on love. For example, marriage, family, and friends all have love at their core. In my early adulthood, I felt very fulfilled. I had plenty to keep me busy and plenty of love in my life. I had a strong love for my husband, my family, my friends, and my job. I didn't realize that something was missing until April 8, 2015, the day my son was born. My life was forever changed on that day.

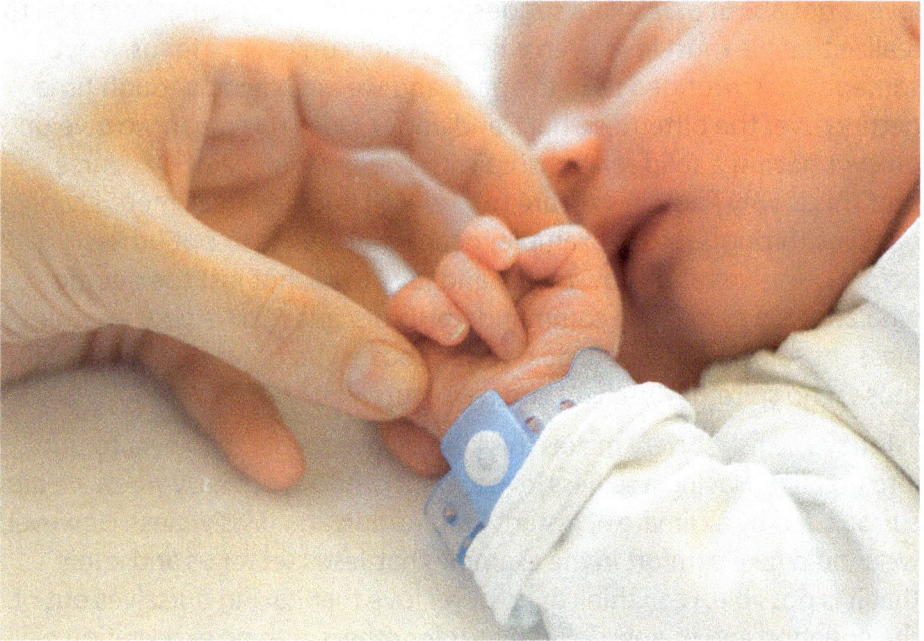

Few things can prepare you for becoming a new mom—the sleepless nights, the emotional roller coaster, and the constant fear and insecurities that come while caring for a newborn. Yet, the most surprising thing that happens *(i.e., the thing that everyone tells you will happen, but you just don't believe until it does)* is that you have an overwhelming love for this little person that goes beyond the boundaries of any love you have ever felt before.

Now that I am a mom, I think of the insurmountable love I feel for my son, and I wonder this: If I can't even put into words the love I feel toward my child, I can't comprehend the love that God has for us, His children. I think back on all the times I have felt "less than," and I am immediately ashamed. We are God's children. Even though we are not worthy of His sacrifice, we belong to Him. As much as we love our spouse, our family, our friends, and our children, none of that holds a candle to God's love for us. With this understanding, we can cultivate some common traits that we should exhibit as we work toward loving others more completely and selflessly.

What characteristics do most of our relationships have in common?

- **Loyalty**—We feel a sense of devotion to those we love.

- **Respect**—We appreciate our loved ones and want to make them feel admired.

- **Trust**—We believe in them and put our faith in them.

- **Connection**—We can relate to them and find a common link that ties us to them.

- **Forgiveness**—We recognize when they stumble and are willing to show mercy.

- **Acceptance**—We can accept them for who they are and are open to their perspective, even if it is different from our own.

If we take these common characteristics and look at what the Bible says, we get a similar definition. "Love suffers long and is kind; love does not envy; love does not parade itself, is not puffed up; does not behave rudely, does not seek its own, is not provoked, thinks no evil; does not rejoice in iniquity, but rejoices in the truth; bears all things, believes all things, hopes all things, endures all things" *(1 Cor. 13:4-7)*.

By taking these important principles and applying them to our current relationships, we show that we have a better understanding of God's love and how we are to mirror that love through our connections with other people, whether it be our family members, friends, church family, coworkers, or complete strangers. "Beloved, let us love one another, for love is of God; and everyone who loves is born of God and knows God. He who does not love does not know God, for God is love" *(1 John 4:7-8)*.

One of the greatest and most frightening parts of being a parent is knowing that you have someone who is constantly looking up to you for guidance and direction. The same is true of us as Christians. The expectation is that we will always do the right thing, and we are examples to others who are looking at us, whether or not we realize it. Because of this, we must not hide our light from others. Building our relationships on God's expectations of how we are to show love will help us keep our light safe from the darkness.

Hide it under a bushel—NO!

I'm gonna let it shine.

Hide it under a bushel—NO!

I'm gonna let it shine.

Let it shine, let it shine, let it shine.

Conclusion

When I was a child singing "This Little Light of Mine," I never thought much about its meaning. Now that I am older, I understand that while it is a song about bringing glory to God by our example to others, it communicates an even greater meaning.

To Fannie Lou Hamer, on a bus ride in 1962, that hymn symbolized hope. It also represented the chance to make a difference in the world. Fannie became a prominent leader in the civil rights movement. Her conviction that society could change for the better was born from her faith in God. I can only imagine, in a time of such oppression, she chose that childhood hymn because it conveyed her belief that even in times of persecution, love can prevail. Jesus taught us this very lesson as he walked on this earth among people who persecuted Him.

Jesus said, "This is My commandment, that you love one another as I have loved you. Greater love has no one than this, than to lay down one's life for his friends" *(John 15:12-13, ESV)*. If we are not willing to heed His command to love with the same devotion that has been shown to us, then what was His ultimate sacrifice for? We are God's children. It is through our light and our steadfast love for others that we bring glory to our Father. Each day brings a new opportunity to let it shine!

Let it shine over the whole wide world,
I'm gonna let it shine.
Let it shine over the whole wide world,
I'm gonna let it shine.
Let it shine, let it shine, let it shine.

Thought Questions

1. How would you define the biblical concept of "love?"

2. How does *agapē* love differ from self-centeredness and sinful desire?

3. List a few practical ways you can "Let it Shine" for others.

4. Why is it so hard to follow the examples set by Jesus when it comes to loving our enemies?

5. What roadblocks are in your way to obtaining the steadfast love that Jesus describes?

6. In today's society, it is sometimes harder to love others in the way we are commanded. Why do you think that is?

7. Are there times when loving others is made easier by today's society?

8. What is one story in the Bible that resonates with you because of its message about love?

Concept Seeds

To begin preparation for the next lesson, please consider the following questions:

Is my attitude characterized by joy? When others look at me, do they see me as a joyous person?

Joy
By April Flowers

Introduction

But the fruit of the Spirit is love, joy, peace, patience, kindness, goodness, faithfulness, gentleness, self-control; against such things there is no law (Gal. 5:22-23, NASB).

But the fruit of the Spirit is love, joy, peace, longsuffering, kindness, goodness, faithfulness, gentleness, self-control. Against such there is no law (Gal. 5:22-23, NKJV).

Paul said, "But the fruit of the Spirit is. . . joy" *(Gal. 5:22)*. For women of faith, joy persists despite life's difficulties. Joy is defined as calm delight, cheerfulness, fullness, great pleasure, or happiness. The word occurs prolifically in Sacred Scripture. We can obtain such wonderful happiness through obedience to the Lord because of the spiritual blessings He provides: "Blessed be the God and Father of our Lord Jesus Christ, who has blessed us with every spiritual blessing in the heavenly places in Christ" *(Eph. 1:3)*. As David exclaims, "Be glad in the Lord and rejoice, you righteous; and shout for joy, all you upright in heart" *(Ps. 32:11)*. Our lives reflect the joy that fills us in the service we give to our Lord, our relationships with our families, our brethren, and those outside the Lord's church.

Joy Comes from the Lord and He Should Be the Recipient of Our Joy

Often, we are surrounded by things that are thought to bring joy. In reality, they are merely passing pleasures designed to satisfy oneself. They lack the depth or sustainability of joy that can only be found in the Lord. When the angel announced the birth of Jesus to Mary, he said, "Do not be afraid, for behold, I bring you good tidings of great joy which will be for all people" *(Luke 2:11)*. What a wonderful blessing that we can still be partakers of the joy that Christ brought when He came in the flesh to this earth. David says, "You will show me the path of life; in Your presence is fullness of joy; at Your right hand are pleasures forevermore" *(Ps. 16:11)*. Why may true joy be found in our Lord? As David declares, we obtain the spiritual, eternal life through Him.

Not only is the Lord the *source* of our joy, but we are also called to rejoice *in* Him. Paul admonishes believers, "Rejoice in the Lord always. Again, I say, rejoice!" *(Phil. 4:4)*. We show our joy by giving glory to God in our worship to Him, and in our daily lives. "You have turned my mourning into dancing; You have put off my sackcloth and clothed me with gladness, to the end that my glory may sing praise to You and not be silent. O Lord my God, I will give thanks to You forever" *(Ps. 30:11-12)*. With all the care and blessings He provides us, we show our thanksgiving by praising Him in our prayers, songs, and actions.

Joy Is Not Situational

Life is full of challenges and can be difficult, but that does not mean that our joy is lost. Instead, our inward joy in the Lord sustains us when the storms of life hit. Philippians is often referred to as the epistle of joy. The noun "joy" and the verb "rejoice" are found sixteen times in this short epistle. Considering Paul's circumstances when he wrote the letter, we are all the more impressed with his attitude of joyfulness while in chains. Imprisonment and even possible death were not capable of stealing his joy. He said, "For to me, to live is Christ, and to die is gain" *(Phil. 1:21)*. This is why Christ called us to lay up treasures in heaven *(Matt. 6:19)*. If that

is where our joy is rooted, then no one can take it from us. If Paul could endure a life of beatings, shipwrecks, perils, hunger, lack of clothing, and weariness *(2 Cor. 11:24-28)* and still find joy, then we can be encouraged under challenging circumstances as well. Consider the words of Job as he dealt with immense amounts of difficulties, "But it is still my consolation, and I rejoice in unsparing pain, that I have not denied the words of the Holy One" *(Job 6:10, NASB)*. We have a choice that can be made as to whether we will go through life with a sorrowful disposition, or we will carry with us an attitude of happiness and gratefulness. It has been said that discouragement is one of Satan's greatest tools. If one allows himself to get so discouraged that he can no longer find the joy in salvation and service to God, then Satan will take hold of his soul, which is a legitimate cause of sorrow.

Joy Is Found through Service

How can we obtain this fruit of the Spirit in a world full of sorrow and pain? First, our joy is found in service to God; next, in service to our fellow brethren and man. Isn't it amazing that when we look for ways to serve others and meet their needs, we are filled with joy ourselves? Paul's last words to the Ephesian elders remind us of this truth: "I have shown you in every way, by laboring like this, that you must support the weak. And remember the words of the Lord Jesus, that He said, 'It is more blessed to give than to receive'" *(Acts 20:35)*.

When we serve with a willing disposition, out of love, it benefits so many: God rejoices in our service and is glorified, the ones we serve are made joyful, and we find joy in helping others. "Therefore if there is any consolation in Christ, if any comfort of love, if any fellowship in the

Spirit, if any affection and mercy, fulfill my joy by being like-minded, having the same love, being of one accord, of one mind. Let nothing be done through selfish ambition or conceit, but in lowliness of mind, let each esteem others better than himself. Let each of you look out not only for his own interests but also for the interests of others" *(Phil. 2:1-4)*. In these verses, Paul describes how he would rejoice to see them united in truth and serving one another's needs. On a children's Bible CD, we have one of the lines of a song gives an acronym for the word joy that summed it up well: **J**esus first, **O**thers second, **Y**ourself last: **JOY!**

Joy Is Found in Our Influence

As we go about our lives as Christian women, it is so vital to carry about us an attitude of joy and contentment because our influence on others can be immense. When we read Proverbs 31, we do not witness a woman who is going about her life with an attitude of sorrow and misery. On the contrary, she is able to do all the things she accomplishes because of her positive attitude. "She shall rejoice in the time to come" *(Prov. 31:25)*. Her hard work and service to her husband and family provided happiness. When our children can see a mother, who goes about her work with an attitude of joy, they are so much more likely to have a disposition of love and kindness. Do we grumble and complain about fulfilling our domestic duties? Will our daughters desire to become homemakers when they are grown, or will they see it as a life of menial tasks and drudgery because of our attitude? We must be an example to our children because they imitate us in so many ways. We can set a tone of happiness and love in our homes by our attitude and disposition.

As we deal with non-Christians, how can we help bring others to Christ if we are filled with anger and discontent? "Let your light so shine before men, that they may see your good works and glorify your Father in heaven" *(Matt. 5:16)*. Others around us will notice how we cope with the various issues life gives us. Perhaps our example of calm joy and happiness will help bring them to Christ.

Conclusion

Let us find great joy in the salvation of Christ and live it out in the actions of our lives. We must look to our perfect example of Christ, as we read in Hebrews 12:1-2. "Therefore we also, since we are surrounded by so great a cloud of witnesses, let us lay aside every weight, and the sin which so easily ensnares us, and let us run with endurance the race that set before us, looking unto Jesus, the author and finisher of our faith, who for the joy that was set before Him endured the cross, despising the shame, and has set down at the right hand of God." As we strive to live a life of joy and contentment here on earth, remember the promise of heaven, where no sorrow at all can invade. "And God will wipe away every tear from their eyes; there shall be no more death, nor sorrow, nor crying. There shall be no more pain, for the former things have passed away" *(Rev. 21:4)*.

Thought Questions

1. What strategies have you used to maintain joy, even during difficult times?

2. Can you think of two scenarios in which the world promises joy, but in the end, cannot deliver?

3. How can a woman of faith "offer" her joy as a gift to the Lord?

4. Please provide at least two verses that reflect this same idea.

5. In your opinion, why does serving others result in joy?

6. Practically, how is it possible to maintain joy for even a full day, much less for a lifetime?

7. Please share examples from Sacred Scripture that help you meet this challenge.

Concept Seeds

To begin preparation for the next lesson, please consider the following question:

Why is it such a challenging thing to find and sustain peace in our hearts, relationships, and congregations?

Peace
By Mary Richardson

Introduction

But the fruit of the Spirit is love, joy, peace, patience, kindness, goodness, faithfulness, gentleness, self-control; against such things there is no law (Gal. 5:22-23, NASB).

But the fruit of the Spirit is love, joy, peace, longsuffering, kindness, goodness, faithfulness, gentleness, self-control. Against such there is no law (Gal. 5:22-23, NKJV).

Peace is one of the most elusive fruits of the Spirit. It is also one of the hardest to maintain. You can easily find *moments* of peace: watching the sun slant through the window while drinking your morning coffee, hearing your children laughing together in the next room, or singing the swelling notes of your favorite song at church. However, what about those other times, when your faith is under fire, when your world has been shaken into chaos, or even when an irritating personality intrudes too often into your life? As Christians, we have a responsibility to promote peace. Let us perceive that peace is a result of our salvation. Finally, may we recognize that peace is our reward.

Definition

Peace may be defined as follows: "a state of mutual harmony between people or groups, especially in personal relations; cessation of or freedom from any strife or dissension; a state of tranquility or serenity; freedom of the mind from annoyance, distraction, anxiety, etc." *(Dictionary.com).*

Promoting Peace

We are told to "pursue the things that make for peace" *(Rom. 14:19)*. It is our responsibility to promote peace: "If it is possible, as much as depends on you, live peaceably with all men" *(Rom. 12:18)*. This command includes "all men." That can be an uphill battle. Ephesians 5:22-33 explains the proper relationship between husbands and wives. Ephesians 6:1-9 goes on to describe other relationships between parent and child and also servants and masters. Our relationship with the government is described in 1 Timothy 2:1-3 and Romans 13:1-7. Our relationships with the elders in the church are depicted in 1 Peter 5:1-5 and Hebrews 13:17. Peace in our relationships with others depends on maintaining our proper roles in those relationships. That is why God, in His wisdom, spent so much time describing the duties and demands of these relationships. Often, we become dissatisfied in our roles, feeling overlooked, unappreciated, and powerless. Sometimes others within these relationships do not fulfill their roles, leading to frustration and resentment. How do we maintain peace?

Peace in Submission

The idea of submission and obedience is prominent in all passages that describe what our relationships must be. While modern American women may not be comfortable with such thoughts, God's wisdom transcends all cultures. As the husband/wife relationship reflects Christ's relationship with His church *(Eph. 5:22-33)*, our obedience to God can serve as a pattern to others. True submission demands selflessness and humility. Most, if not all, conflicts result from one or more parties insisting on their rights, their way, or something that will benefit themselves. Philippians 2:3-4 says, "Let nothing be done through selfish ambition or conceit, but in lowliness of mind let each esteem others better than himself. Let each of you look out not only for his own interests but also for the interests of others." In verses 5-11, Paul describes Jesus's humility as the supreme example for us. Whenever you feel you are not receiving your due, whenever you become resentful

because someone isn't treating you with respect, think of this: Jesus, equal with God, Creator of the heavens and the earth, made Himself to be the lowliest of men, to take a painful and humiliating death, to save the very people who were mocking Him as He died. He did not have to do that; He could have stopped it at any time. Yet, He humbled Himself for our benefit. Keep that in your mind at all times. Compare your behavior to Jesus's example and humble yourself. Remember, it is "better to be of a humble spirit with the lowly than to divide the spoil with the proud" *(Prov. 16:19)*.

Peace in Salvation

However, peace is not merely a responsibility in our relationships or a characteristic of the complete Christian. Peace is a way of describing the result of salvation. In baptism, we are reconciled with God. "For it pleased the Father that in Him" *(i.e., in Jesus)* "all the fullness should dwell, and by Him to reconcile all things to Himself, by Him. . . having made peace through the blood of His cross. And you, who once were alienated and enemies in your mind by wicked works, yet now He has reconciled in the body of His flesh through death" *(Col. 1:19-22)*. Though we were separated from God by our sins *(Isa. 59:2)*, God offers peace through the person of Jesus *(Eph. 2:14-18; Rom. 5:1)*. The whole story of the Bible is the story of the conflict sin created between God and man and the lengths God took to allow us to make peace with Him.

Peace as a Reward

Finally, peace is a personal reward. This is the "peace of God, which surpasses all understanding" *(Phil. 4:7)*. Isaiah wrote, "The work of righteousness will be peace, and the effect of righteousness, quietness and assurance forever" *(32:17)*. Righteousness here is contrasted with the wicked and their lack of peace *(Isa. 48:22; 57:19-21; 59:8)*. Romans tells us, "For to be carnally minded is death, but to be spiritually minded

is life and peace" *(8:6)*. Not that this peace is earned by us, but when we obey the gospel in faith and continue in it, we can have this peace. The story of Peter walking on water is an excellent example of how to attain and maintain this peace. As long as Peter kept his focus on Jesus, he was able to walk on water. "You will keep him in perfect peace, whose mind is stayed on You" *(Isa. 26:3)*. When Peter noticed "that the wind was boisterous, he was afraid" *(Matt. 14:30)*. As the waves distracted Peter, so the conflicts and troubles of the world can distract us.

Conclusion

Nevertheless, this promise of peace does necessarily apply to our external earthly circumstances. Jesus told His disciples, "Peace I leave with you, My peace I give to you; not as the world gives do I give to you. . ." *(John 14:27)* and "These things I have spoken to you, that in Me you may have peace. In the world you will have tribulation; but be of good cheer, I have overcome the world" *(John 16:33)*. David understood this peace in times of chaos. Take time to read Psalm 46, which describes the world in chaos *(vv. 2-3)* and God's supreme control *(vv. 5-11)*. How can we keep this sense of peace when our own lives are in upheaval? David tells us, "Be still and know that I am God" *(Ps. 46:10)*. Philippians 4:6 tells us that to obtain this peace that surpasses all understanding, "In everything by prayer and supplication, with thanksgiving, let your requests be made known to God." Meditate on the promises God has given us, knowing that He is able to perform all that He has promised. "He who overcomes shall be clothed in white garments, and I will not blot out his name from the book of life, but I will confess his name before My Father and before His angels" *(Rev. 3:5)*.

Thought Questions

1. How do peaceful relationships bring glory to God?

2. How does the peace of knowing your sins are forgiven contrast with knowing your sins are not forgiven?

3. To what extent does the peace of God protect women of faith from the world's chaos?

4. Can you share at least two Bible examples that demonstrate inner peace despite external difficulties?

5. Throughout each day, what method do you use to reset your heart and mind to peace?

6. Do you ever need to do this more than once during the day?

7. In your own words, explain why knowledge of the sovereignty of God always provides peace.

Concept Seeds

To begin preparation for the next lesson, please consider the following questions:

What situations in the life of Jesus tested His patience? What can His longsuffering teach you about facing things in your life with patience?

Patience
By Bridget Huber

Introduction

But the fruit of the Spirit is love, joy, peace, patience, kindness, goodness, faithfulness, gentleness, self-control; against such things there is no law (Gal. 5:22-23, NASB).

But the fruit of the Spirit is love, joy, peace, longsuffering, kindness, goodness, faithfulness, gentleness, self-control. Against such there is no law (Gal. 5:22-23, NKJV).

We live in a "want it now, get it now" technology-infested culture. A simple push of a button instantly mobilizes fast-food take-out, conveniently bagged groceries, and that "needed" pair of shoes, available online and delivered tomorrow. Patience, however, is more difficult to find. Our society has cleared the way for this fast-paced tempo while leaving our spiritual visions of patience quite cloudy. We want patience, but we want it now. How do we rectify our deep need for patience amid our love affair with convenience?

Enduring without Complaint

To be patient, as defined by *Merriam-Webster*, means to "bear pains or trials calmly or without complaint." In our text, in Galatians 5, the term longsuffering is used and is defined as "patiently enduring lasting offense or hardship." In theory, patience shouldn't be hard to master, right? Just sit, wait, and watch as things fall into place—their rightful place. Just sit tight and wait. Theory is one thing; reality is another. When our desires and expectations don't manifest themselves in a "timely" manner, we often become irritable, agitated, and unable to practice patience. Sometimes circumstances create difficulty in our lives, and we just want it to stop. Now! Yet, sometimes the difficulty doesn't stop. Sometimes it gets worse. Sometimes the hardship lasts and lasts. Then what?

Unfortunately, life is full of trials thrown at us daily. As Christians, we are expected to be patient in tribulation—it's part of our commitment to Christ. James 1:12 tells us that enduring trials through patience puts us on track to receive the crown of life. As Christians, we're called to put on longsuffering *(Col. 3:12)*. Romans 8:24-30 reveals to us that our hope of heaven requires so much patience—it's impossible to make it there without it! The question then is: how do we gain patience when both our cultural training and the natural tendency is to be impatient?

Enduring with Trust in God

Patience, as a facet of the fruit of the Spirit, emerges from trust in God. Being patient must be about trusting Him in all things. It's hard for us to see the bigger picture as mere humans when things don't pan out exactly how we want. Yet, where is our focus? Is our focus on our Father or the earthly things around us? Is our focus on the here and now, or on better things to come? As God declared to Jeremiah, He has a plan for us! A plan to give us hope and a future *(Jer. 29:11)*! When we are forced to wait on God's perfect plan for us, we are tested. When we worry, anticipate, or act as if we know better, do we not realize that this is insulting to our wonderful, all-knowing Creator? However, when we wait on God, we learn patience and show that we trust Him and His plan for us *(Jas. 1:2-4)*.

Pursuing Patience

Patience doesn't come automatically. In 1 Timothy 6:11, we are told to *pursue* righteousness, godliness, faith, love, and gentleness. . . and patience. Because it has become cliché over time, the truth that

"patience is a virtue" may cause us to assign it to a lower rank in our minds. Rather than just parroting platitudes about patience, let's pursue it! Long lines, slow cashiers, and traffic jams may not inspire us to pursue anything but our comfort. Yet, those are the precise times when we should remember we were called, not to a life of ease, but to pursue patience. God commands patience, not irritability.

Patience cannot be assigned lesser importance in our daily lives when our heavenly Father commands it. You will emulate Christ by showing yourself understanding and patient to others around you. What a beautiful command patience actually is!

Examples of Patience

Thankfully, God generously provides many examples patience in His word *(2 Pet. 3:9)*. Our heavenly Father doesn't want us to fail; that's for sure. Accordingly, He has given us everything we need to succeed!

Abraham

We all know the three famous promises made to Abraham in Genesis 12 by heart: *land, seed*, and a *great nation*. Take to heart, too, that even though Abraham never saw the fulfillment of all God's promises, he remained steadfastly faithful to God. Hebrews 11:8-12 reminds us that God led Abraham on a long, round-about journey. Although it might have seemed aimlessly in his eyes, Abraham trusted God, loving Him so much that he kept patiently following. Through it all, trust and patience went hand in hand—just as they should in our lives.

Jesus

Now, let's move on to someone that should be a little more relatable to us—Our Lord and Savior, Jesus Christ. He's the One to whom we look for guidance in everything we do, especially when it comes to patience. Reflecting upon Matthew 27:11-14, we recognize that Jesus could have easily refuted Pilate and stood up for Himself; yet, He did not do so. Although this immediately makes us think of His self-control, it also displays His immense amount of patience. He patiently pursued the plan His Father had for Him. Jesus trusted God's perfect plan and refrained from attempting to alter that plan, even though He recognized the awaiting agony. Despite having the power to change the course and alter the plan, He didn't. Think about the momentous patience that was required! By pursuing God's plan to the end, so that His last words on the cross were, "It is finished!" Jesus demonstrates the possibilities and the power of patience available to us as we face difficult situations.

Other Examples

Many biblical characters offer us encouragement on this subject: Job in Job 42, Joseph in Genesis 37-46, and the father of the prodigal son in Luke 15:11-24. Isn't it comforting to know that when our patience is tested, we can look to the pages of God's word for guidance in forbearance and wisdom to wait in times of adversity?

Conclusion

Despite our fast-paced world, as children of God, we learn to wait on the Lord, displaying lives of patience, even in times of turmoil and worry. We look to the Bible for guidance and comfort on this subject.

Thought Questions

1. List some situations that try your patience.

2. Using a Bible dictionary or Greek lexicon, provide a meaningful definition of patience.

3. Come up with a definition of patience that relates to your life.

4. It's so easy to lose sight of what should be most important in our lives. What do you do, or what could you do to prevent this? Be specific.

5. List all the positive outcomes that come from being patient with someone else.

6. List a Bible figure that also displayed patience and briefly explain what challenges he or she faced.

7. Briefly explain how you plan to apply what we've learned in this lesson to your life.

Concept Seeds

To begin preparation for the next lesson, please consider the following question:

What are some specific characteristics that demonstrate kindness?

Kindness
By Nichola Peterson

Introduction

But the fruit of the Spirit is love, joy, peace, patience, kindness, goodness, faithfulness, gentleness, self-control; against such things there is no law (Gal. 5:22-23, NASB).

But the fruit of the Spirit is love, joy, peace, longsuffering, kindness, goodness, faithfulness, gentleness, self-control. Against such there is no law (Gal. 5:22-23, NKJV).

Kindness, more than simply what you *do*, is what you *don't do*, how you think, and what drives your behavior. Just as it's challenging to prevent the delicious filling from bubbling out of a baking pie, the

kindness in our hearts shouldn't be containable but should burst forth, showing the hidden places of our soul, bubbling from our hearts flavoring our words, thoughts and actions.

The Wife, a Fruitful Vine

Your wife will be like a fruitful vine in the very heart of your home (Ps. 128:3).

Does this describe you? Does it depict the way that you habitually conduct yourself within your family? Does your kindness fill "the heart of your home" with warmth, or is your presence a dark shadow of bitter unpleasantness? Are you a nourishing, flourishing presence or a fountain of woe and withering words?

Who among us does not wish to be the heart of our home? We were created for this role, but sin creeps in; anger takes root. As women of faith, we must choose kindness.

Defining Kindness

Kindness Does No Harm; Kindness Meets the Need

Kindness is a fruit we value and recognize, but finding a precise definition is difficult. This challenge is compounded by the number of Greek and Hebrew words that are translated kindness in Sacred Scripture, each with its distinctive shade of meaning. In our present context, Paul uses *chrēstotēs* to communicate the concept of kindness. While this word generally signified "usefulness" or "helpfulness," it is defined as "*(1)* uprightness in one's relations with others, uprightness; *(2)* the quality of being helpful or beneficial, goodness, kindness, generosity; *(a)* of humans; *(b)* of God" *(BDAG, 1090)*. HELPS Word-studies describe it as "useful kindness" that "refers to meeting real needs, in God's way, in His timing. . . the Spirit-produced goodness which meets the need and avoids human harshness *(cruelty)*, excellence, uprightness." It brings to mind the Hippocratic oath that medical professionals take to "above all, do no harm," but a further step is required—positive action to meet a need.

Kindness Derives from Deity

We will focus on the three uses of the word *chrēstotēs* since that is the rare word chosen by the Holy Spirit to describe this aspect of the fruit of the Spirit. In Galatians 5:22, kindness *(chrēstotēs)* depicts a facet of the visible fruit produced in the life of one who has been born of the Spirit. Kindness is a fruit "of the Spirit," so it is born from the Spirit. The other two uses of this term in the New Testament further confirm that this kindness is an essential attribute of God Himself. God is kind. So those born of His word find their own character transformed into this image as well. Romans 11:22 contrasts God's kindness toward the saved with His severity towards the fallen: "Therefore, consider the goodness *(chrēstotēs)* and severity of God. . ." Titus 3:4 describes how the kindness *(chrēstotēs)* of God toward man appeared: "Not by works of righteousness which we have done, but according to His mercy He saved us, through the washing of regeneration and renewing of the Holy Spirit, whom He poured out on us abundantly through Jesus Christ our Savior."

Getting to the Heart of the Issue

"Ugh! You're taking forever!" These unkind words from the sweet innocent mouth of my three-year-old daughter made me ashamed. She was saying to me what I say to her when I am trying to rush her out the door or into bed. My daughters and husband are the people I love most in this world, and yet, I am often sharp with them over small insignificant things. I suspect that I am not alone in this.

Our familiarity and proximity with our loved ones make them natural victims of our unkind moments. We go home and leave the rest of the world for a few hours a day, but not our family. Our children are there screaming at 10 p.m. when we just want to fall into the bed. Our husband is there with needs and perceived shortcomings when we are feeling overwhelmed. Our guard is down, and what we say and do

often reflects poorly on our inner self. We may even excuse ourselves for occasional slip-ups with our family because we are kind in all our other interactions. In these moments, when we are naked of pretense and manifest the actual state of our heart. If we can't be kind to those we love most, the chances are good that the kindness we show those in our extended family, church family, friends, coworkers, and those we pass on the street or in the store is a weak facade. This is how we go from being a friendly driver to a crazy lady shouting at the tail lights of a car that cut us off. It is why we get caught up in gossip at work. It is why our friend *("Bless her heart")* is getting on our nerves. It is why we allow a rift to form in our extended or church family.

How do we bring kindness into familiar and everyday relationships so that, from there, it permeates our every interaction? How can we make our best behavior our only behavior?

Vital Humility

Genuine kindness cannot exist where there is no love for our fellow man. Another character trait vital to nourishing kindness is humility. It is hard to find offense in anything our fellow man can say or do when we see it considering our failure before God and our reliance upon His grace. Unfortunately, that perspective is easy to lose. Suddenly, we see every infraction as a personal injustice and give in to unkindness. More than not considering ourselves "better" than anyone else, we must humbly consider ourselves less important than others if we intend to be kind in all situations.

The disciples were busily arguing about who was the Lord's MVP. Yet, He, their Rabbi and Redeemer, humbly and kindly washed their feet. They missed an opportunity for kindness because of their pride, but Christ did not. He had already humbled Himself to leave heaven and walk among them. He now humbled Himself to clean their filthy feet. Soon, He would humble Himself to die on a cross and bear all of our disgusting sins *(Phil. 2:5)*. Certainly, this is the greatest act of love and kindness in all of human history.

I don't know why His disciples and I struggle to let go of our need for importance, but we must do so to be like Christ and subsequently be kind. Until we do, we'll continuously neglect kindness while we argue about our importance. Paul makes this clear in his letter to the Philippians: "Let nothing be done through selfish ambition or conceit, but in lowliness of mind let each esteem others better than himself. Let each of you look out not only for his own interests but also for the interests of others" *(Phil. 2:3)*.

The Apple Farmer

My father-in-law, Ron, grows delicious apples. He works long hours with his trees, ensuring weeds are not choking them and thinning down small fruits to ensure a healthy harvest. He spends his evenings planning how best to protect the trees from diseases and bugs that will destroy them. I grew up on land that had apple trees, but they didn't receive any care. As a result, the fruit on my trees had unsightly blemishes outside and worms inside. When cultivating kindness, we can't treat our hearts like wild apple trees. It's easy to pray for kindness and hope it will arrive in a pretty box with a bow.

Unfortunately, true kindness will not come easily. If we try faking kindness externally rather than putting in the work to develop a heart of kindness, our pretense won't hold up under testing any more than my wormy apples would pass a quality inspection. When we pray for our hearts to produce kindness, we need to recognize that we are making a lifetime commitment to cultivating that fruit. Fruit farmers often have to wait and work for years before the trees are mature enough to harvest. Let that sink into your mind. The farmer has spent thousands of dollars on trees and countless hours planting, pruning, weeding, and caring for those same trees, and yet for several years, he does not get a real harvest. He might get an apple here and there the first year. Then the second year, a few apples will grow, but not enough to sell. Yet, the

farmer keeps nurturing those little trees, and in a few years, they are laden with fruit. We need to pray and work and be patient. We will start seeing kindness grow in us, but it will probably be years before we can say it is a natural reaction in all situations. When we attain kindness, we must remain vigilant that it stays rooted in our hearts, just as farmers continue to nurture trees even after they are mature.

Cultivating Kindness

We can do several things to protect our fruit of kindness from the blight of bitterness. As we study kindness in Scripture and honestly examine our hearts *(internal triggers)*, let us look for the roots of unkindness and bitterness, in order to root them out *(Heb. 12:15; 1 John 3:20; Job 13:23)*. We also need to examine our lives and see why we are struggling with kindness *(external triggers)* and thin out those things. This could mean letting go of excessive commitments that overwhelm us to the point we snip at others or neglect opportunities to be kind. It could mean we stop watching our favorite show because of the unwholesome attitudes of characters that foster and feed our unkindness *(Gal 6:7-8)*. It could even mean spending less time with "friends" who encourage us in unfruitful behavior *(1 Cor 15:33)*.

Planning for Success

Ron doesn't start his day/week/year without a plan, or he would otherwise fail to bring in a healthy crop at harvest. How can we expect to develop kindness, a much more delicate fruit, by accident? Recently, we brought my daughter's Power Wheels car to a playdate. During the week leading up to the visit, I explained how she was getting an opportunity to be kind and how sharing makes everyone happy. We discussed potential scenarios and correct responses. At the playdate, she was generous, never fought for a turn, but enjoyed watching her cousins drive her car. Is my daughter a sharing guru? Not at all. She simply had a plan for kindness in a potentially challenging *(to a three-year-old)* situation. In our lives, we clearly cannot plan for every trying situation, but for some, we have plenty of warning and are remiss if we go in unprepared. For those unexpected moments, when unkindness rears its ugly head, we should be armed with Scripture to remind us how to defeat it.

First Comes Love

"Love, joy, peace, patience, kindness. . ." God, who is all-wise, inspired these words. I believe He ordered them intentionally with love as our starting point. It is nearly impossible to find a biblical example of kindness that does not also exemplify love. Out of the abundance of His love for humanity, God shows kindness. God is love *(1 John 4:8, 16)*, and His resulting actions manifest kindness.

Especially poignant is His kindness in sending Jesus to save us. Ephesians 2:7 states "that in the ages to come He might show the exceeding riches of His grace in His kindness toward us in Christ Jesus." This point is made again in Titus 3:4-6, which says, "When the kindness and the love of God our Savior toward man appeared, not by works of righteousness which we have done, but according to His mercy He saved us, through the washing of regeneration and renewing of the Holy Spirit, whom He poured out on us abundantly through Jesus Christ our Savior."

Jesus, the Ultimate Example

Jesus Christ gave up heaven and took on humanity to show us kindness. His every action stemming from love, He poured out kindness on all humanity. humanity. We are called to our sinful, difficult, unkind fellow man with kindness because we are also that same sinful fellow man. Jesus's kindness transcended *(more accurately, transcends)* age, race, religion, lifestyle, social status, and gender. Jesus died for us all.

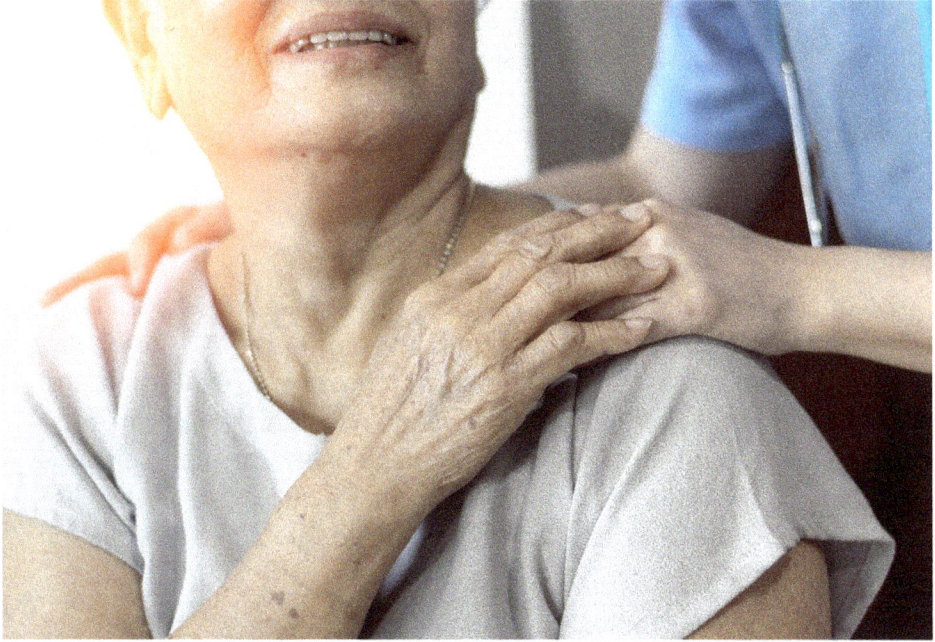

Transcending Age

His compassion for the widow in Nain, who would be destitute in her old age after the death of her son, moved Jesus to raise him from the dead *(Luke 7:11-17)*. His tender words, "do not weep," were undoubtedly balm to her aged heart.

Jesus's invitation to children, "Come to Me" *(Matt. 19:14)*, would have had a similar effect on those pure, tender, young hearts. Jesus's kindness to these people who had no voice in society, and certainly no way to repay Him, must have left a lifetime impression.

Transcending Social Boundaries

"Will you give me a drink?" Jesus's humble query startled the Samaritan woman at the well. After all, she *was* a Samaritan and a woman. Why would this Jewish man deign to drink water from her bucket that was contaminated by social boundaries? Yet Jesus, desiring her salvation, spoke, and without compromising truth or kindness, He told her that He knew about her sins. Still, He cared for *her* and wanted to give her living water. Because of this simple, magnificent act of kindness, she and her acquaintances believed *(John 4:7-42)*.

Choosing Useful Kindness

The good Samaritan in Luke 10 was moved to help the Jewish man lying wounded beside the road, despite everyone else crossing the road to avoid him. Assisting this stranger was inconvenient, expensive, and possibly dangerous, yet he saw a desperate need and humbly filled it, generously sharing his blessings. For all he knew, the man he was helping hated Samaritans, but that didn't factor into his decision. His decision to choose kindness had been made long before the situation presented itself.

Just as he is as good an example of useful kindness, as the Pharisees in Matthew 15, are examples of useless kindness. Their actions looked good, even kind. They were giving money to God, perhaps more than the ten percent that was required. That money was being used for good, but Jesus rebuked them. He knew their hearts and motives. They were intent on avoiding the responsibility of caring for their elderly parents *(a command of God)*, so much so that they gave a little extra to God so they could show their empty wallets while remarking with feigned sadness, "What you would have gained from me is given to God" *(Matt. 15:5)*. Like the Samaritan, they had decided beforehand, but any "kindness" they manifested was useless and small compared to the need they intentionally left unfulfilled.

Conclusion

From giving Peter a chance to undo his three denials *(John 21:15-17)*; to praying for the souls of those crucifying Him *(Luke 23:34)*; to interacting with all kinds of unclean and diseased people *(Luke 8, 17)*, Jesus models active, useful, unstoppable kindness that should drive our every interaction. Does an honest look at your daily interactions similarly reveal the fruit of kindness in your heart, or does an uglier image emerge? Is the blight of anger choking out your kindness? This does not have to continue! Stop feeding the weeds in the garden of your heart. Do not give place to anger or allow the devil a foothold in your heart *(Eph. 4:26-27)*. Of all earthly creatures, I fear snakes the most. This spring, I pulled out all the weeds in my yard that would give snakes places to hide. It took me hours and four wheelbarrow loads of weeds to complete my task, but I was amazed by the results. Not only was there no place for snakes to hide, but my yard looked much tidier. That is what God tells us to do with our hearts. Pull out all the weeds of evil, put in the work until there is nowhere for the devil to hide in your heart. Then kindness can flourish. Like a tree freed of choking, you will begin to flourish in ways you did not believe possible.

Sources

BDAG = Arndt, William. et al. *A Greek-English Lexicon of the New Testament and Other Early Christian Literature.* Chicago: University of Chicago Press, 2000.

HELPS Word-studies: "Chrēstotēs." *BibleHub.com.* https://biblehub.com/str/greek/5544.htm.

Thought Questions

1. Share an example of kindness that you have witnessed. What stood out to you the most?

2. In your opinion, what would "kindness" look like when it proceeds from a proud heart?

3. How does love empower greater acts of kindness?

4. In our culture, what makes it difficult to reach out to destitute people or families?

5. Can you find any help or answers from God's word to help us do better?

6. What is the seed that produces anger?

7. Explain how anger interferes with kindness.

8. How should kindness transcend the barriers that otherwise serve to isolate us from others?

Concept Seeds

To begin preparation for the next lesson, please consider the following question:

How will the world's concept of goodness differ from what is seen in Scripture?

Goodness
By Cynthia Dann

Introduction

But the fruit of the Spirit is love, joy, peace, patience, kindness, goodness, faithfulness, gentleness, self-control; against such things there is no law *(Gal. 5:22-23, NASB)*.

But the fruit of the Spirit is love, joy, peace, longsuffering, kindness, goodness, faithfulness, gentleness, self-control. Against such there is no law *(Gal. 5:22-23, NKJV)*.

What is goodness? As we partake of God's goodness, repentance results *(Rom. 2:4)*, filling hungry souls *(Ps. 107:9)*. As God's goodness, revealed through His seed, the word of God *(1 Pet. 1:23)*, takes root and develops in hearts of faith, the fruit of goodness emerges. Anyone can dutifully perform good works. However, goodness that pleases God derives from a heart that is under the transformative power of God's good news, the gospel. Cultivating this fruit of the Spirit, we "fulfill all the good pleasure of His goodness" *(2 Thess. 1:11)*.

Definition

In the New Testament, "goodness" *(agathōsunē)* signifies that "positive moral quality characterized especially by an interest in the welfare of others" *(BDAG, 4)*. Goodness may be defined as "uprightness of heart and life" *(Thayer, 3)*. It may be described as doing the right thing for the right reason. Perhaps goodness exhibits not only in the kindlier aspect but also in stronger, sterner qualities of an ideal character. Goodness never compromises with sin or error, yet contains the strength to overcome evil. Deeper than the mere outward performance of good works, goodness reaches to the inward character of the heart of faith and manifests in conduct transformed by the gospel of Christ.

Attributed to God

Only God is truly and thoroughly good *(Matt. 19:17; Mark 10:18)*. As Creator, He created all things good *(Gen. 1:31)*, displaying externally in His creation the innate goodness of His character *(Pss. 27:13; 33:5)*. In response to Moses's request to see God, the goodness of God radiated as His glory, passing by the cleft of the rock *(Exod. 33:17-23)*. God's goodness abounds *(Exod. 34:6)*, enduring continually *(Ps. 52:1)*. He shares His goodness as a gift to the faithful *(Ps. 21:3; 1 Kings 8:66)*.

Attributed to Christ

While present as God in the flesh on earth, Jesus manifested the goodness of the character of God, committing no sin *(Heb. 4:15; 1 Pet. 1:18-19; 2:22; 1 John 3:5)*. As the Word, He overcame evil with good through relying on the revealed, written will of God *(Luke 4:1-13)*. His ministry comprised going about doing good *(Acts 10:38)*, which is clearly defined by His works. He performed miracles, healing many incurable diseases and ailments, casting out demons and unclean spirits, and raising people from the dead. Almost as astounding as these miracles, Jesus showed a depth of compassion, even for strangers and sinners. He gently forgave sins and patiently taught all who came to Him, including even those who stood in opposition to Him.

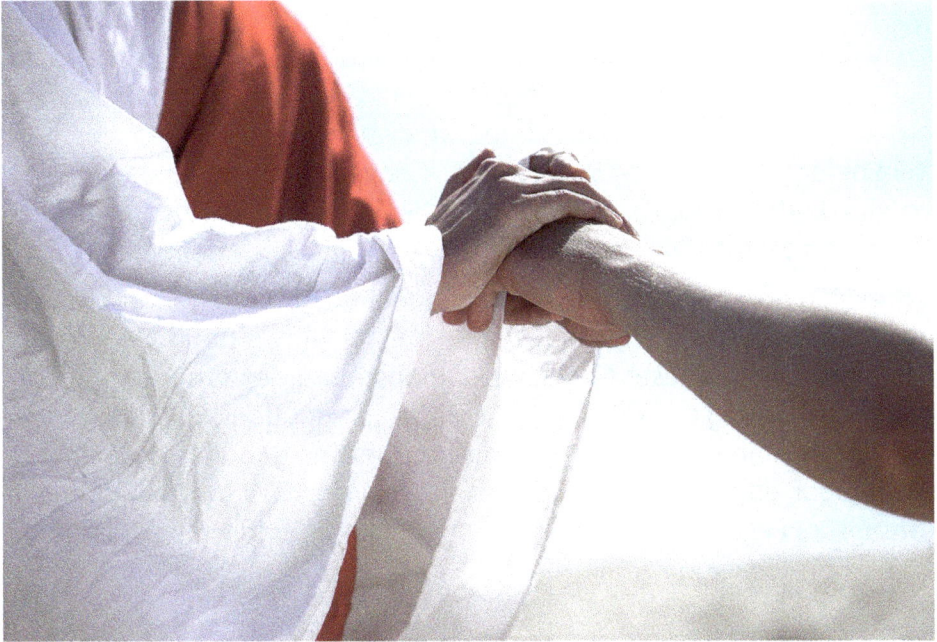

How Can I Acquire This Goodness?

It Is Available

Goodness is attainable. God expects followers of Jesus to acquire the character of goodness, equipping us through the instruction of the Holy Spirit. A submissive mindset enables us to receive and believe the teaching of God like our brothers and sisters in Thessalonica *(1 Thess. 2:13)*. As we develop a heartfelt desire to practice goodness *(Col. 3:2)*, the all-sufficient word provides nourishment *(Jas. 1:21)*, bringing forth good treasure *(Matt. 12:33-37)*.

Pursuing Goodness

Developing the fruit of goodness involves the intentional pursuit of God's way. Filling our minds with good things that are approved by God, our hearts are transformed so that He approves our character *(Phil. 4:8)*.

Our first steps toward righteousness turn our hearts, minds, and feet away from evil. Yet, goodness must go much further. If we repent of sin but fail to fill our lives with the substance of God's ways and words, the production of God's fruit is hindered, and we may end up even worse than before *(Matt. 12:43-45; 2 Pet. 2:20)*. Conversely, by continually walking in the goodness that is taught by God, we can overcome even the power of evil *(Rom. 12:21)*.

Pursuing goodness leads to good conduct that is both honorable and observable *(1 Pet. 3:13)*. By choosing to imitate what is good, clearly exhibited for us by Jesus Christ, we demonstrate by external action that our hearts belong to God *(3 John 11)*. Pursuing goodness involves more than intent. It involves more than desire. Pursuing goodness requires work, labor, effort, and striving *(Rom. 2:10; Eph. 4:28)*. It involves doing *(Gal. 6:10; 1 Pet. 3:11)*. It involves proving *(Rom. 12:2)*. It involves clinging *(Rom. 12:9; 1 Thess. 5:21)*.

Recognizing Impediments

Goodness is an aspect of the Spirit's fruit, produced by the Spirit's seed, the word of God *(1 Pet. 1:23)*. If something other than goodness is consistently exhibited in one's life, it can only mean that other seeds are present and producing fruit. "A good man out of the good treasure of his heart brings forth good, and an evil man out of the evil treasure brings forth evil" *(Luke 6:45)*. Have you cleared the soil of your heart to make room for the seed, the word, so as to manifest the fruit of God's goodness? Or is the debris of the cares of this world choking out the life of God's seed in you? What about your view of others? A good heart rejoices in God's just approach and fair treatment to all, but developing an "evil eye" towards others chokes the growth of God's seed in us *(Matt. 20:15)*. If we allow the continual choking of the implanted word, production fails, God's goodness turns away, and we are cut off from Him *(Rom. 11:22)*.

Bible Examples of Goodness

Jesus

Our Savior always performed the right actions from the right heart. His uprightness of heart showed righteous indignation as He cleansed the temple of those who had perverted its purpose *(Matt. 21:12-13)*. After powerfully resetting the temple's purpose as a house of prayer and a place for worshiping God, Jesus moved on to other essential acts of goodness. His compassion, gentleness, and true love toward humanity were exhibited in healing the sick, blind, and lame, casting out demons, and proving His authority as the Son of God *(Matt. 21:14)*.

Hezekiah

As king of Judah, Hezekiah walked in goodness, performing righteousness before the Lord. Because he respected the law of the Lord, Hezekiah cleansed the temple, restored proper worship, and kept the Passover. In every work that he performed, Hezekiah's actions radiated from a committed heart. Do we have this kind of courage to teach, admonish, and correct errors that creep in among God's people? Do we have the uprightness of heart to do our part in resetting the service and worship of God to the pattern He desires and commands?

Barnabas

A "good man, full of the Holy Spirit and faith" *(Acts 11:23-24)*, Barnabas portrayed noteworthy goodness among the thousands of people who were being added to the Lord. This "son of encouragement" *(4:36)* spurred many to continue diligently and with purposeful hearts in their pursuit of God's goodness. Among those whose lives he changed by genuine and resolute kindness was the newly converted Saul/Paul. When doubtful brethren in Jerusalem hesitated to accept Paul, Barnabas took him to the apostles, sharing the truth concerning Paul's conversion and his undeniable boldness for the Lord in Damascus. Do we exhibit this same goodness toward the newly converted and babes in Christ? Do we encourage their continuance and growth? Sadly, we can easily fall into the "evil eye" attitude of the early laborers in the vineyard *(Matt. 20:1-16)*, which manifests as impatient judgment and distrust. However, by a conscious decision and deliberate action, we can stir up the fruit of goodness and display a God-trusting love that "believes all things" *(1 Cor. 13:7)*.

Tabitha

Also known as "Dorcas," this godly woman was full of good works and charitable deeds *(Acts 9:36-43)*. She unselfishly lived her life in service to others, using her own hands to create and fashion garments for them to wear. Not all good works stem from a heart of kindness. Not every act

of charity is goodness. Genuine goodness starts in the heart, and, over time, extends into external actions. In Tabitha, the people recognized genuine sincerity of heart and eager service. Those who were impacted by her goodness dearly loved her.

Roman Saints

Described by Paul as being "full of goodness" *(Rom. 15:14)*, the saints in Rome filled their hearts and minds with the knowledge of the Scriptures. From Scripture-saturated hearts, spiritual growth arose, which enabled them to admonish one another effectively. When we learn God's word, are we motivated to do good by encouraging others to grow? An upright heart can't remain unconcerned with the spiritual wellbeing of others. Goodness endeavors to perform the right actions from a right heart.

How Does Goodness Affect Our Lives?

The prophet Jeremiah spoke of God's faithful people, declaring, "Therefore they shall come and sing in the height of Zion, streaming to the goodness of the Lord. . . their souls shall be like a well-watered garden, and they shall sorrow no more at all" *(Jer. 31:12)*. The prophet's words paint a beautiful picture of the benefits of being a vessel filled with the goodness of the Lord. Goodness positively affects every relationship in our lives, including our relationship with God, the church, our spouses, our children, and the world.

Our Relationship with God

We enter a relationship with God when we repent of sin and obediently answer the call of the gospel of Jesus Christ. As we study and grow, we begin to fill our lives with simple acts of goodness, adding virtue to faith. It is important to note that God's offer of goodness is only for His obedient children *(Ps. 23:1-6)*. Every command of God is beneficial. Christians are blessed with every spiritual blessing, including the fruit of goodness *(Eph. 1:3)*. As we learn what is pleasing to the Lord, we necessarily make changes so that God can produce the fruit of goodness in us *(Eph. 5:9-10)*.

Our Relationship with God's Family

The Bible offers wonderful instruction concerning how we should conduct ourselves in our relationships with our brothers and sisters in Christ. We are to be of the same mind toward one another *(Rom. 12:16)*. We are to examine the Scriptures, reminding ourselves and others to hold to the pattern and share in all good things with those who teach us *(Gal. 6:6)*. We should endeavor to "do good to all men, especially those who are of the household of faith" *(6:10)*.

Our Relationship with Our Spouse

For those who choose to enter into the marriage covenant, both parties anticipate being good to one another. As the husband loves his wife as Christ loved the church, he will fulfill her needs. As the wife lovingly submits to the husband's assigned role of leadership, she will fulfill his needs *(Eph. 5:22-23)*. Titus 2:3-5 instructs older women to teach what is good, including loving submission to their own husbands. Proverbs 31:1-12 depicts the virtuous woman as one who does her husband good and not evil all the days of her life.

Our Relationships in Our Homes

As mothers, we are instructed to love our children, desire good for them, help train them in the nurture and admonition of the Lord, and teach them to pursue goodness and purity in their lives *(Titus 2:3-5; Prov. 22:6; 31:26; Eph. 6:4)*. Mothers must be aware that they are expected to model goodness for their children. Modeling goodness externally naturally flows from mothers who fill themselves with God's goodness.

Our Relationship with the World

As Christians, we shine as lights in the world. "The fruit of the Spirit consists in all goodness, righteousness, and truth," and the light of this goodness necessarily exposes the unfruitful deeds of darkness, rather than participating in them *(Eph. 5:8-11)*. As children of light, our interactions with the world entrust vengeance to God, so that we repay no one evil for evil, we regard good things in the sight of all, and we overcome evil with good *(Rom. 12:17, 21)*.

Conclusion

Pursuing goodness leads to repentance *(Rom. 2:4)* and fills the hungry soul *(Ps. 107:9)*. Furthermore, God's goodness is reserved for those who fear and trust in Him *(Ps. 31:19)*. The fruit of goodness simply exhibits externally the goodness of God that fills the upright heart. Anyone can work a good work. Nonetheless, the goodness that pleases God derives from a heart that is under the transformative power of God's good gospel. Cultivating this fruit of the Spirit, we "fulfill all the good pleasure of His goodness" *(2 Thess. 1:11)*.

Sources

BDAG = Arndt, William. et al. *A Greek-English Lexicon of the New Testament and Other Early Christian Literature.* Chicago: University of Chicago Press, 2000.

Thayer, Joseph Henry. *A Greek-English Lexicon of the New Testament.* New York: Harper & Brothers, 1889.

Thought Questions

1. What is the relationship of good works to goodness?

2. How are they the same?

3. How are they different?

4. What kinds of activities pollute the heart of a woman of faith?

5. Why will these influences diminish the ability to exhibit goodness?

6. What is the opposite of having a unified heart and action? Please provide at least two verses that address this issue.

7. In your opinion, why is it necessary to actively pursue goodness?

8. How does the goodness of Jesus affect your life today?

Concept Seeds

To begin preparation for the next lesson, please consider the following question:

How is faithfulness exemplified by God the Father, the Son, and the Holy Spirit?

Faithfulness
By Kate Mitchell

Introduction

But the fruit of the Spirit is love, joy, peace, patience, kindness, goodness, faithfulness, gentleness, self-control; against such things there is no law (Gal. 5:22-23, NASB).

But the fruit of the Spirit is love, joy, peace, longsuffering, kindness, goodness, faithfulness, gentleness, self-control. Against such there is no law (Gal. 5:22-23, NKJV).

The writer of Hebrews declares, "Now faith is the substance of things hoped for, the evidence of things not seen" *(Heb. 11:1)*. Faithfulness, an action-based quality, results from continual application, not simply a one-time effort. Ongoing loyalty, continuing support, and abiding trust, or full-of-faith-ness, demonstrates this spiritual fruit.

A Faithful Creator

Above all, God Himself deserves our faithfulness in our relationship to Him. God exhibits His faithfulness to us in His awesome creation.

He is faithful in the sunrise: "The LORD'S loving kindnesses indeed never cease, for His compassions never fail. They are new every morning; great is Your faithfulness *(Lam. 3:22)*.

He is faithful in the seasons: "While the earth remains, Seedtime and harvest, cold and heat, winter and summer, and day and night shall not cease" *(Gen. 8:22)*.

He is faithful in His handiworks: "By faith, we understand that the worlds were framed by the word of God, so that the things which are seen were not made of things which are visible" *(Heb. 11:3)*. His marvelous works show His handiwork, and the universe faithfully maintains day by day like clockwork.

A Faithful Savior

From the beginning until the end, Jesus demonstrates faithfulness: "Forever, O Lord, Your word is settled in heaven. Your faithfulness endures to all generations" *(Ps. 119:89-90)*. The things of faith are invisible for now, but we recognize that they are real through our faith in God. 2 Corinthians 5:7 says: "For we walk by faith, not by sight."

His Love

"Having loved His own who were in the world, He loved them to the end" *(John 13:1)*. Despite failings and lack of understanding in the disciples, Jesus faithfully loved.

His Service

"I am willing" *(Matt. 8:3; Mark 1:41; Luke 5:13)*. Undeterred by exhaustion or exasperation, Jesus served faithfully—making no excuses.

His Sacrifice

"For this reason the Father loves me, because I lay down my life, that I may take it again. No one takes it from me, but I lay it down of my own accord. I have power to lay it down, and I have power to take it again; this charge I have received from my Father" *(John 10:17-18)*. Facing the world's darkest moment, Jesus willingly offered Himself as a sacrifice for sins, providing us with the hope of salvation.

Faithful Relationships

In Marriage

The husband and wife relationship in a marriage is an example to which most of us can relate. Within the joys and challenges of required faithfulness, God teaches us about Christ and the church: "This is a great mystery, but I speak concerning Christ and the church" *(Eph. 5:32)*.

In the Church

Our faithfulness is based on Romans 10:17, which says, "Faith comes by hearing, and hearing by the word of God." What we hear and how we apply it is crucial to our spiritual lives and the lives of those around us. Our minds retain, remember, and recall what we hear and see. Our faith depends on this backing every day of our lives. Yet, we need to make sure our "backup system" is full of God's truths and words. We should pray for the *desire to grow* in faithfulness by looking into His word *(Ps. 119:11)*: "Thy word have I hid in my heart that I might not sin against thee." The author of Hebrews tells us to "give the more earnest heed to the things we have heard, lest we drift away" *(2:1)*.

Ancient Faith

   Many ancient believers exemplified faithfulness *(Heb. 11)*. They were known for their faithfulness towards God in their individual ways. "By faith Abel offered a more excellent sacrifice" *(Heb. 11:4)*. In contrast, his brother Cain offered a sacrifice outside of faith and was rejected by God. So, just offering a sacrifice did not automatically give him divine approval. We must take this to heart with our attitude towards our devotion to God. Merely attending worship and going through the motions does not mean we will be pleasing to God. We must have faithful and obedient hearts, as did the heroes of Hebrews 11. By faith, Enoch had a pleasing faith, which allowed him to go directly to God without dying. "Without faith it is impossible to please Him, for he who comes to God must believe that He is, and that He is a rewarder of those who diligently seek Him" *(Heb. 11:6)*. Noah had a saving faith by faithfully following patterns from God's plans, saving himself and his family from the wicked world. Abraham had an obedient faith, faithfully waiting on the Lord to fulfill his promise to him that through him, Messiah the Seed, would come. Sarah had a submissive faith, yielding to the Lord because "she judged Him faithful who had promised" *(Heb. 11:11)* a child in her old age. Moses had an enduring faith, forsaking "Egypt and looked to the reward from Him who is invisible" *(Heb. 11:27)*. All of these, and more, obtained a good testimony concerning their faithfulness, believing an unseen God who had given promises to them. They patiently waited for God to fulfill His words, and God kept all of His promises. These all died without seeing the promise fulfilled in their lifetime; yet, they remained faithful and did not succumb to despair, nor allow their faith to be quenched. What excellent examples of faithfulness!

Daily Faith

The way we handle daily decisions will show where our heart is and where our faithfulness lies. We will be known by our "fruits" *(Matt. 7:16-20)*, false or sincere, good or bad. Faithfulness has no hypocrisy in it *(Jas. 3:17)*. It is pure: "Even so, every good tree bears good fruit, but a bad tree bears bad fruit" *(Matt. 7: 17)*. Worldliness and bad influences lead us in the wrong direction, impeding our growth, making our fruit bad. These works of the flesh will, in the end, be revealed—be sure that our sins will find us out *(Num. 32:23)*. Bad fruit will show itself in the time of harvest.

Determined Hearts

So, where does this faithfulness begin? It begins first in our hearts. "The foundation for all that is possible for a man to believe, for all the faith that you can exercise is the word of God. There is no other source and no other power that is able to plant faith in the heart of an individual" *(Cogdill, 28)*. We must nourish our hearts and keep them healthy by feeding on spiritual food. For if we become "sick," we need to search out Jesus, the "Great Physician" *(Matt. 9:35)*. His remedy requires much prayer *(Jas. 5:16)*, study *(2 Tim. 2:15)*, watchfulness, and determination to overcome the wiles of the devil. "For our adversary the devil walks about as a roaring lion, seeking whom he may devour" *(1 Pet. 5:8-9)*. We are to "Resist him, steadfast in the faith." We show our faithfulness to God by resisting the devil through our alliance to Christ, who promises to help us.

Dedicated Actions

We only have control over the faith in our own individual lives as we sojourn among the wicked in this world. We are teaching others in ways that we might not realize. As some have said, "We may be the only Bible that others see and read." We must be on guard at all times and keep a tight rein on our thoughts, speech, tongue, and actions. Our actions can speak louder than do our words. Strive always to be a good example as we do not know the hour of our departure from this earth. Our faithfulness and obedience to our Lord is our pathway to heaven.

Wilting Habits

Resistant attitudes creep into our lives, hindering the growth of faithfulness. Laziness, tiredness, rebellion, and apathy cause a once-flourishing faith to wilt. Self-satisfied assumptions such as, "I don't need to learn anymore" or "I've already heard all this before" only extinguish faithfulness. Pride stunts growth, shading humility and blocking the light of the gospel from shining through our lives. Boasting of oneself as "somebody" actually stunts actual growth *(Acts 5:36)*. Such attitudes destroy the fruit of faithfulness and spread a killing disease within the roots of our faith.

Nourishing Habits

Assemble

The healthy plant of "faithfulness" shines forth as a motivated faith, habitually obeying God's commandments. As an example, we demonstrate loyalty to God and faithfulness within His body by "not forsaking the assembling of ourselves together" *(Heb. 10:25)*. "Our stress should be on living the Christian life daily, on the everyday walk with God. Attending the assembly is but one phase of our life. If we are living the life of faith, we shall not neglect the privilege and the duty of assembling with the brethren" *(Bales, 73)*. Fellowship with brethren strengthens, edifies and encourages ourselves and others as we exhibit faithfulness to God. A closer walk to God during the week helps us fruitfully grow healthier in our walk down that "straight and narrow way" *(Matt. 7:14)*. Sadly Jesus tells us, "few there be that find it." We must diligently strive to walk in this way. "If we walk in the light, we have fellowship one with another, and the blood of Jesus Christ His Son cleanses us from all sin" *(1 John 1:7)*.

Unify

Therefore, having been justified by faith, we have peace with God through Jesus Christ" *(Rom. 5:1)*. We unify within the faith, generating this peace that first originated in the mind of God, then was delivered by Jesus and the Holy Spirit. Our Lord prayed for the unity for all believers, "that they all may be one, as You, Father, are in Me, and I in You; that they also may be one in Us, that the world may believe that You sent Me" *(John 17:21)*. Faithfulness shines forth through unity.

Self-Check

Is this fruit of faithfulness maturing in your life? "But also for this very reason, giving all diligence, add to your faith virtue, to virtue knowledge, to knowledge self-control, to self-control perseverance, to perseverance godliness, to godliness brotherly kindness, and to brotherly kindness,

love. For if these things are yours and abound, *you* will be neither barren nor unfruitful in the knowledge of our Lord Jesus Christ" *(2 Pet. 1:5-10)*.

- **Faith:** "I believe God."
- **Virtue:** high moral standard
- **Knowledge:** true knowledge from God
- **Self-control:** the subjection of desire to one's will
- **Perseverance:** do, and keep on doing
- **Godliness:** devout commitment to God
- **Brotherly Kindness:** kind benevolence to others
- **Love:** acting for another's good

"For so an entrance will be supplied to you abundantly into the everlasting kingdom of our Lord and Savior Jesus Christ" *(2 Pet. 1:11)*. What sweeter words could ever be heard than "Well done thou good and faithful servant"? Are we striving to obey, maturing the fruit of faithfulness, and living in hope of entrance into the everlasting kingdom of Jesus?

Sources

Bales, James D. *The Faith Under Fire*. Shreveport, LA: Lambert Book House, 1967.

Cogdill, Roy E. *Faith and the Faith*. Bowling Green, KY: Guardian of Truth Foundation, 1986.

King, Sr., Daniel H. *The Bible Text Books: Hebrews*. Athens, AL: Truth Publications, 2008.

Thought Questions

1. How is the fruit of faithfulness displayed in a Christian's life?

2. Please take a moment to look up the definition of the Hebrew word *hesed (Strongs #H2617)*, often translated "lovingkindness." Find at least two verses where this term is used.

3. How does God's lovingkindness *(hesed)* impact His people?

4. In your opinion, does Jesus's sacrificial death demonstrate more faithfulness to God or more faithfulness to His people?

5. If the fruit of faithfulness is absent in a Christian woman's life, what does that look like on any given day? Please find at least two verses to illustrate.

6. If the fruit of faithfulness is abounding in a Christian woman's life, what does that look like on any given day?

7. Please find at least two verses to illustrate.

Concept Seeds

To begin preparation for the next lesson, please consider the following question:

What is the difference between weakness *(or timidity)* and meekness *(and gentleness)*?

Gentleness
By Erin van Niekerk

Introduction

But the fruit of the Spirit is love, joy, peace, patience, kindness, goodness, faithfulness, gentleness, self-control; against such things there is no law (Gal. 5:22-23, NASB).

But the fruit of the Spirit is love, joy, peace, longsuffering, kindness, goodness, faithfulness, gentleness, self-control. Against such there is no law (Gal. 5:22-23, NKJV).

When we think about "gentleness," sometimes we think of it as a disposition of certain people. In other words, some people are just naturally gentle, and others are not. Although we do all have different personality types, gentleness is something we all can, and must, develop as children of God. If we live in the Spirit, we will walk in the Spirit of gentleness.

What Is Gentleness?

A gentle person must first be humble. If we are not humble, it is impossible to be gentle. When we are humble, it will produce the fruit of gentleness. A gentle person will be forgiving, merciful, and considerate of others.

Considering these definitions, we recognize that gentleness is a characteristic of the heart. It is the heart and attitude behind kindness and good deeds. We can be kind and good to others, but if it is done without the spirit of gentleness, we have missed the whole point.

Gentleness *(prautēs)* describes a disposition that is even-tempered, tranquil, balanced in spirit, unpretentious, with passions under control. The word best translates as "meekness," which is not as an indication of weakness, but of power and strength under control. One who possesses this quality will pardon injuries, correct faults, and rule her own spirit well. Gentleness is due to a person's conscious choice, and recognition of God's sovereign rule.

Thus, gentleness, humility, compassion, and forgiving others go hand in hand. In many verses, gentleness, humility, and forgiving others are mentioned together *(Eph. 4:1-3; Col. 3:12-13)*. You can't have one without the others.

What Produces Gentleness?

Looking Back to the Ancient Pattern

We must seek spiritual nourishment. Studying God's word and Jesus's example, meditating on it, and looking inward are essential steps towards growing and producing gentleness. We look into the perfect law of liberty, which teaches and trains us to be the type of Christian that indeed observes our own heart, and applies gentleness in our lives *(Jas. 1:23-25)*.

Looking Inward with Personal Humility

Manifesting humility is essential to producing gentleness. If we truly have a sense of our moral insignificance and manifest a humble attitude of unselfish concern for others' welfare, we will treat people with gentleness. If we remember where we have come from and what God has done for us, it can help us treat others with gentleness.

"Remind them to be. . . gentle" *(Titus 3:1)*. Paul reminds us that we are all sinners. Christ made an amazing sacrifice for us while we were still sinners, leaving no room for pride. Remembrance of Christ's sacrifice

helps guide us towards developing the humility we need to produce the fruit of gentleness. People can easily tell if a person thinks she is "better than" others. We need to truly realize that no matter how moral we are, we are no better than anyone else nor deserving of any greater grace. If we can truly understand and grasp the significance of what Jesus did for us, we cannot help but exhibit gentleness towards others.

We need to make sure that we are not like the Pharisee that "prayed thus with himself, "God, I thank You that I am not like other men. . . ." Instead, we strive to emulate the tax collector who humbly cried out, "God, be merciful to me, a sinner!" *(Luke 18:9-14)*.

Sometimes we mistakenly have this same attitude about or towards others. Yet, we recognize that Jesus warned against such arrogant and self-righteous attitudes, saying, "Everyone who exalts himself shall be humbled, and he who humbles himself will be exalted" *(Luke 18:14)*.

Looking Upward to Jesus's Example

Jesus Himself manifests humble gentleness. Looking to His ways cultivates within us a heart producing gentleness. In every aspect of His life, Jesus depicts gentleness in His humble birth, in His merciful interactions with those enslaved to sin, in His unassuming entrance on a donkey *(Matt. 21:5)*, in His easy yoke with a light burden *(Matt. 11:28-30)*, and in His forgiving plea from the cross: "Forgive them. They know not what they do" *(Luke 23:34)*.

Therefore, let us listen to His teaching. At its core is true humility and gentleness. He teaches that a gentle person forgives others as He has forgiven us. In the parable of the unforgiving servant in Matthew 18:21-35, Jesus magnifies the necessity of remembrance of the great debt He paid on our behalf. From a heart that remembers, we, in turn, forgive others. Reading through this parable, we witness the complete injustice of the unforgiving servant demanding repayment. Despite receiving overwhelming pardon of his debt, he mercilessly went after one profoundly less entrenched than himself. We may fall into this exact

sinful mindset. Listening to Jesus trains our hearts always to remember how our King dealt with us. In thankfulness, we do the same for others, looking inward with self-application and remembrance.

True Compassion Manifests Gentleness

Toward Lost Sinners

In John 8:1-11, Jesus demonstrated gentleness towards sinners when He showed compassion on them. He had compassion for the woman that was caught in adultery. In this familiar passage, Jesus provides an amazing depiction of gentleness, especially contrasted with the Pharisees. Jesus's gentle response toward the woman silently but powerfully magnified the sinfulness of her accusers. He led with gentleness and compassion. His attitude toward sinners reflects genuine compassion, giving us a perfect example of how we can look at and treat others.

Toward Wandering Sheep

In Matthew 9:36, Jesus led with gentleness, prompted by a heart of compassion. When He considered them, Jesus rose above the annoyances of earthly shortcomings, recognizing their true condition: sheep without a shepherd. With that mindset, He set out to be a shepherd to them. He hoped to lead them out of aimlessness, into purpose. Also, He wanted to show them how to turn away from sin and choose the safety of God's way. Sadly, despite all His efforts, most turned away from Jesus's leadership and chose their way instead.

Toward the Sick and Suffering

In Matthew 14:14, Jesus healed the sick because of His compassion. Can you imagine being the Creator of humanity? Then, when you came to visit, your creation is miserable and nearly destroyed with sickness?

Jesus did not ignore or overlook them. He did not turn away in disgust. Instead, He exhausted Himself day after day, healing and helping them. "When Jesus went out He saw a great multitude, and He was moved with compassion for them and healed their sick" *(Matt. 14:14)*.

Toward Hungry Travelers

In Mark 8:2, Jesus had compassion on the hungry multitude before He performed the amazing miracle of feeding them. He recognized that their journey had taken them far away from access to necessary food. Even though the people were following Jesus the whole time, the trip still became difficult, and they did not have any way to feed themselves. Instead, He abundantly provided to fill their hunger.

Toward All Humanity

In Romans 5:8-10, we learn that Jesus's compassion did not end once He ascended to heaven. It extends even until today, even to us. Without a Savior, we have no hope for forgiveness and no hope of sharing a relationship with God. Jesus saw that condition and made a sacrifice that would reach to every sinner—then, and now.

Impediments to Gentleness

The biggest weeds that prevent gentleness from growing are pride and self. It is one thing to understand what gentleness is and see when others aren't acting that way, but we need to look inward and apply it to ourselves. Pride prevents us from seeing fault in ourselves but magnifies fault in others. As we look at them through pride, focusing on faults, we will not treat them with gentleness. If we are self-centered, we won't see the value in others' lives or feel compassion for others, making it nearly impossible for us to treat people with gentleness.

Almighty God Leads Gently

It is comforting to know that God is gentle. He is our loving Father that knows and wants what is best for us. Often, this conflicts with what we might think we want or need. Our heavenly Father is not a cold-hearted Overlord or cruel Master, who is waiting for us to stumble so that we can be punished. Instead, He loves and cares for us, gently leading us to embrace His truth and submit our lives unto His will *(Ps. 23: Isa. 40:11; John 3:16)*.

God Expects His People to Be Gentle

God has always expected His people to be gentle or meek *(Jas. 1:21)*. The meek realize that God is in control and realize their need for God and His grace. They have a dependence on God. We should humble ourselves to accept God's truth unconditionally, just as small children accept and believe everything their parent might tell them *(Matt. 18:3-5)*. A gentle person will humbly accept God's word.

In the Church

Gentleness does not overlook sin or neglect to help and correct a fellow Christian that is caught up in sin. The approach we use and how we correct someone, including our underlying attitude, matter to God. We must seek to restore erring brothers in a spirit of gentleness and love, or we may find ourselves just as much in the wrong. It is amazing to see how Galatians 6:1-4 teaches and guides us to have the correct attitude towards restoring a fellow Christian. God wants us to restore the erring while simultaneously realizing that we are nothing and are no better than the one being restored. Even when correcting, we are to be peacemakers and not the type of people that just push to "prove our point" or "win" an argument.

In Marriage

God has given us the best marriage counseling we could ever get. We shouldn't be surprised that God has the answers to our marriage since He created us and marriage itself! Often in life, we find it most challenging to demonstrate gentleness to the people with whom we share the closest relationship. Our attitude can influence our spouse for good; we need to be understanding to our spouse and his views, and we need to put other's needs before our own *(1 Pet. 3:1-7; Eph. 5:25-28)*.

In Parenting

Gentleness is described as a nursing mother cherishing her children *(1 Thess. 2:7)*. When we demonstrate gentleness toward our children, we teach them the gentleness of God. When we respond to our baby's cries, we model how our loving Father also responds to our cries. When we put our needs aside, caring for our children's needs before ourselves, we model how God takes care of our needs.

I was blessed to be the oldest of many siblings, so I experienced the gentleness of a mother and witnessed the gentleness she showed my younger siblings. Both my parents were excellent examples of putting children's needs before themselves. Growing up with the security of parental love was indeed a blessing and helped me understand and feel more secure in God's love for me. They had high expectations and were consistent. They weren't gentle because they had made no demands, but because they made reasonable demands with love.

Jesus put us before Himself when He sacrificed Himself for us on the cross. We strive to model the same form of teaching and instruction, Jesus is not a vindictive taskmaster, waiting for us to make mistakes, but through loving care and gentle guidance, He imparts lessons of truth.

We must teach our children to possess these qualities God wants us to exhibit. As parents, we exercise the most significant influence on their development and learning, greater than any school or educational institution, or even the church.

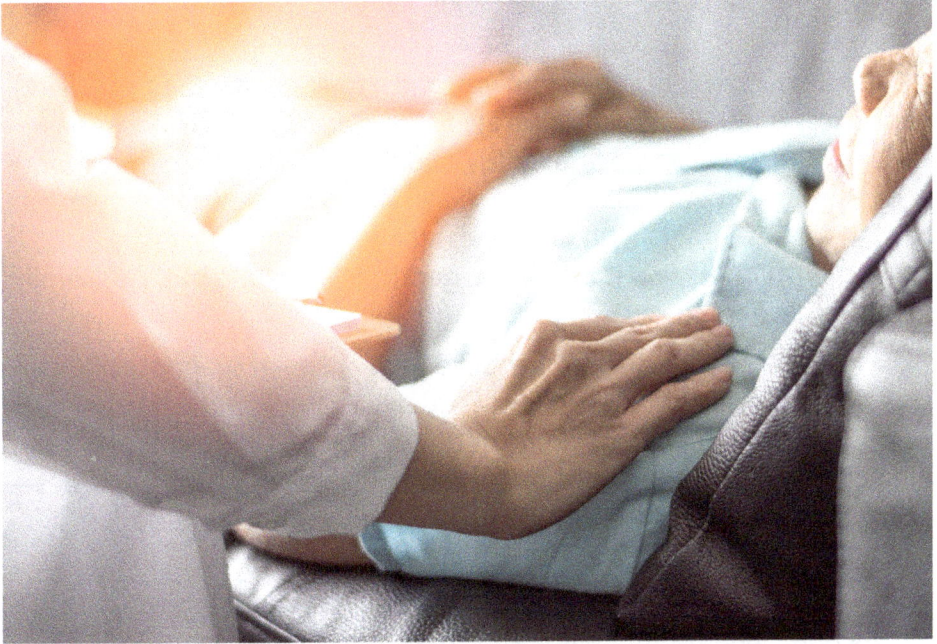

I remember my mom teaching me to think about the feelings of others from a very early age. Whether it was someone mistreating others or me, she always stressed that they might be in a hard situation and to think about the other person and have compassion for her.

In the World

Another lesson I still remember is to feel compassion for people who do not know God yet. Sometimes as Christians, we forget that one of the most important jobs we have is to let our light shine to the world and teach others about Christ *(Matt. 5:16)*. Showing gentleness to others is a great way to let your light shine. It matters how we treat those whom we encounter every day. We need to see people as God does—precious souls that need Him. As peacemakers, we show compassion.

We can be on the right side of all the moral issues *(which is vitally important)*, yet without the spirit of gentleness. An insistent prideful spirit does not correctly represent Christ, nor does it shine His light.

Conclusion

A gentle person is humble, forgives, and shows compassion. Applying gentleness is not always easy. We all have different circumstances and people in our lives. Some find it easy to be gentle with their close friends and family members *(because they share a loving relationship)* but find it hard to treat strangers with gentleness *(because they share no personal connection)*. Others find it easy to be gentle to everyone but their family members.

We need to train ourselves to choose gentleness—regardless of the situation or person with whom we are dealing. Think of the person with whom you have the most trouble getting along and to whom you have difficulty demonstrating gentleness. Try to see him or her as God does—as a precious soul that He loves.

Remember that I am not perfect and that I need God and His grace. Remember what Christ has done for me. Remember that God loves the person and values that persons' soul. Remember that God expects me to demonstrate the same gentleness He showed me. Remember that it matters to God how we treat each other.

This is the process that helps me have gentleness towards others. At first, it will be very purposeful and might even seem forced, but practicing these steps over and over helps develop an appropriate automatic response.

You shall love the Lord your God with all your heart, with all your soul, and with all your mind and you shall love your neighbor as yourself (Matt. 22:37-39).

This is true gentleness. First, depending on God; then, showing gentleness to others. Even though gentleness is a challenge, it is possible: "I can do all things through Christ who strengthens me" *(Phil. 4:13)*.

Thought Questions

1. How does a recognition of God's sovereignty help produce a gentle spirit?

2. Why is it tempting to pridefully correct people who are actively sinning against God?

3. Can you think of a marriage situation in which gentleness *(by either the husband or the wife)* might profoundly alter the relationship for good? What verses echo this principle?

4. Why does it matter whether a mother is gentle towards her children? Can you think of a Bible example *(either positive or negative)* that demonstrates this need?

5. In your opinion, why is a recognition of your imperfections helpful in developing a gentle spirit?

Concept Seeds

To begin preparation for the next lesson, please consider the following questions:

Who is someone in my life that I respect for their ability to practice self-control? What could I do to imitate his or her example?

Self-Control
By Paula Kingsley

Introduction

But the fruit of the Spirit is love, joy, peace, patience, kindness, goodness, faithfulness, gentleness, self-control; against such things there is no law (Gal. 5:22-23, NASB).

But the fruit of the Spirit is love, joy, peace, longsuffering, kindness, goodness, faithfulness, gentleness, self-control. Against such there is no law (Gal. 5:22-23, NKJV).

I love snickerdoodles, especially right out of the oven. The cinnamon sugar, crunchy outside, and soft, chewy center—delightful! I enjoy them so much that I often lose track of how many I have eaten. "Just one more," I think, as the timer rings, and I pull the piping hot tray from the oven. Embarrassingly, I have been known to eat so many that a stomach ache ensues. On those occasions when the "just one more" has turned into too many more, I wonder, "Why didn't I stop myself? What was I thinking?" While this example may seem trivial, we engage in similar battles with our flesh every day. In Romans 7:15, the apostle Paul said, "For what I am doing, I do not understand. For what I will to do, that I do not practice; but what I hate, that I do." Paul was not talking about snickerdoodles when he made that statement. Yet, when it comes to controlling our desires, whether over-indulgence, impulsive behavior, poor time management, or the like, we can all empathize with his thoughts.

We have come in our study the final aspects of the fruit of the Spirit: self-control. In a world of high-speed internet, two-day shipping, movies on demand, and Instant Pots, is it any wonder that we need self-control? While I believe we would all like to see more restraint in our society as a whole, I am not sure many of us fully realize the deficiency of self-control in our personal lives. Typically, we view the lack of self-control as it is displayed in destructive dependencies or reckless, irrational behavior. However, for most of us, the shortage of self-control is exposed in our day-to-day choices and struggles. Will I control my attitude when my children are not behaving as they ought? Will I put my trust in God through difficult situations or be overcome with worry? Will I choose to study God's word, or peruse Facebook? Will I be snippy with my tongue when I feel wronged or seek to view the issue from the other perspective? Will I eat the entire tray of snickerdoodles? It is these types of decisions that reveal our real level of self-control. As women desiring to *walk by the Spirit*, we must take a serious look at self-control, the role it plays in our spiritual life, and then we must evaluate where we stand.

What Is Self-Control?

At first glance, understanding this ninth characteristic of the fruit of the Spirit seems quite obvious: Simply, it is the control of self. The question arises, what do we need to control, why do we need to regulate it, and how are we to do so? *Webster* defines self-control as "restraint exercised over one's own impulses, emotions, or desires." The Greek word *egkrateia*, translated "self-control" in Galatians 5:23, signifies "restraint of one's emotions, impulses, or desires, self-control" *(BDAG, 274)*. It is "the virtue of one who masters his desires and passions, especially his sensual appetites" *(Thayer, 166-167)*. Its root, *kratos*, conveys the idea of might, power, or strength. A self-controlled woman rules over or governs herself. She is strong in character, willfully keeping her emotions, cravings, and impulses in check.

Why Do We Need Self-Control?

Remember, we are at war, battling against Satan seeks to devour us *(1 Pet. 5:8)*. We are at war with the world and its lusts: "The lust of the flesh, the lust of the eyes, and the pride of life. . . is of the world" *(1 John 2:16)*. We also battle against our own bodies. Our flesh stands in opposition to our spiritual nature. "For the flesh lusts against the Spirit, and the Spirit against the flesh; and these are contrary to one another, so that you do not do the things that you wish" *(Gal. 5:17)*. Peter exhorts us to "abstain from fleshly lusts which war against the soul" *(1 Pet. 2:11)*. We are at war.

It Helps Us Maintain Perspective

Keep cravings in perspective. As we cultivate self-control, we will be able to maintain a spiritual focus. A failure to practice self-control leads to focusing on the flesh. "For those who live according to the flesh set their minds on the things of the flesh, but those who live according to the Spirit, the things of the Spirit" *(Rom. 5:8)*.

The Israelites lost their focus when they yielded to an intense craving for meat in the wilderness *(Num. 11:4-6)*. There was nothing wrong

with wanting meat, or a change of diet. However, they obsessed over this craving, allowing it to grow so strong that they yielded to their craving and changed their perspective. They blamed God and forgot His promises and provision. They lashed out at Moses. They fooled themselves into thinking their appetite for meat was a necessity.

Esau did the same thing when he sold his birthright to Jacob for a bowl of stew *(Gen. 25:29-34)*. Being famished, he gave into his flesh and failed to see the future benefit of his birthright.

Fleshly desires can seem so intense at times. However, if we do not actively take charge of our passions, our passions will control us. When we allow the insignificant to become a priority or permit enjoyable freedoms to become enslaving, we lose our focus. Instead, may we seek to be like Jesus, "who for the joy that was set before Him endured the cross" *(Heb. 12:2)*. Cravings come and go, but God faithfully and completely provides for every need.

It Helps Guard Us from Sin

Sin seeks to rule us. Self-control enables us to rule over sin, standing firm against the schemes of the devil *(Eph. 6:11)*. God warned Cain, "Sin lies at the door; and its desire is for you, but you should rule over it" *(Gen. 4:7)*. As James 1:14-15 declares, each one of us "is tempted when he is drawn away by his own desires and enticed. Then, when desire has conceived, it gives birth to sin; and sin, when it is full-grown, brings forth death." Failure to control our desires gives way to sin, allowing it to rule.

Solomon illustrates how self-control fortifies, comparing it to the walls of an ancient city. "Whoever has no rule over his own spirit is like a city broken down, without walls" *(Prov. 25:28)*. City walls safeguarded its inhabitants from being overrun by robbers or enemy nations. Without walls, they would be defenseless against their foes. In the same way, we are defenseless against temptation when we fail to exercise self-control. By practicing self-control, we do not "give place to the devil" *(Eph. 4:27)*. Self-control defends our spirit.

It Enables Growth

Self-control upholds all facets of spiritual fruit in us. It has been asserted that self-control is the crowning attribute or capstone of the nine aspects of the Spirit's fruit. Without it, all other characteristics cannot be fully present in our lives. How can we show gentleness if we do not control our tongues? How can we be faithful if we are unwilling to restrain our desires? How can we manifest love if we are unable to get a grip on our anger? To grow the other aspects of the fruit of the Spirit, we must keep our flesh in check. Self-control foundationally supports the Spirit's fruit in us.

Mastery of self increases fruitfulness. Peter also stresses the importance of developing self-control, listing the Christian graces. For us to become partakers of the divine nature, we must diligently add self-control to our list of ever-growing Christian graces:

Now for this very reason also, applying all diligence, in your faith supply moral excellence, and in your moral excellence, knowledge, and in your knowledge, self-control, and in your self-control, perseverance, and in your perseverance, godliness, and in your godliness, brotherly kindness, and in your brotherly kindness, love (2 Pet. 1:5-7).

It is not enough to believe and know what is right. We must develop the skill of self-control, putting righteousness into practice. Building self-control enables perseverance to the goal. "For if these things are yours and abound, you will be neither barren nor unfruitful in the knowledge of our Lord Jesus Christ" *(2 Pet. 1:8)*. To mature productively in the kingdom, we cultivate this attribute. Self-control increases fruitfulness.

Seven Keys to Cultivate Self-Control

Thankfully, we strive for a different kind of self-control than is observed among those in the world. It is not a girding up of our *own* strength and will-power for the sake of becoming wealthier, healthier, or more successful. Instead, it involves looking to God for strength, aligning our desires with His will, and focusing on the reward set before us. Does this mean it will be easy? No, but it will be rewarding!

Developing self-control is a continual process, not something achieved overnight, by next week, in six months, or even in several years. Nevertheless, moment by moment, day by day, as we seek His will, self-mastery grows.

Define Your Powerful "YES"

Gary Henry states, "Self-discipline comes from having a hope that means enough to us that we refuse to give it up. We find the strength to say 'No' only when we have a powerful 'Yes' burning within us" *(Jan. 17)*.

Focus like Moses. Moses also ruled over himself when he chose to suffer rather than enjoy the pleasures of sin because he was focused on the reward *(Heb. 11:24-26)*. Consider Jesus. Laying aside all encumbrances, let us run the race with endurance *(Heb. 12:1-3)*.

Press on like Paul. Manifesting self-mastery in all things, let us run the race with patience and press toward the goal *(1 Cor. 9:24-27; Phil. 3:12-14)*. What is your powerful "YES"?

Think on Purpose

With what do I fill my mind? Where is my attention focused? How do I seek to be entertained? We must "keep" *(our)* "heart with all diligence, for out of it spring the issues of life" *(Prov. 4:23)*. To cultivate self-control, we must start with our thoughts.

Paul urges us to bring "every thought into captivity to the obedience of Christ" *(2 Cor 10:5)*, and to "set your mind on things above, not on things on the earth" *(Col. 3:2)*. He warns, "For to be carnally minded is death, but to be spiritually minded is life and peace" *(Rom. 8:6)*. In Philippians 4:8, the apostle provides a litmus test for the things on which our minds should dwell: "Finally, brethren, whatever things are true, whatever things are noble, whatever things are pure, whatever things are lovely, whatever things are of good report, if there is any virtue and if there is anything praiseworthy—meditate on these things." We must choose to rule over our thoughts.

Get into the Word

"Draw near to God, and He will draw near to you" *(Jas. 4:8)*. Of all the things we can do, this is paramount. Unfortunately, many of us neglect it. We must be in the word daily! I should see God's word as being more valuable than gold and sweeter than honey *(Ps. 19:10)*. Without self-control to read and study God's word, to meditate on it, and pray to Him, it is impossible to have self-control in other areas of our lives. Set a timer on your phone! Link Bible study/reading to something else you do every day *(perhaps before a meal?)* so that you won't forget. Do whatever it takes to immerse yourself in God's word and build your relationship with Him. In so doing, our desire to follow God will increase, and our fleshly desires will decrease.

Crucify Self

As Irvin Himmel said, "The practice of self-restraint requires submission to God and denial of self" *(12)*. Just after the list of the fruit of the Spirit in Galatians 5:24, Paul instructs, "crucify the flesh with its passions and desires." Paul says, "I have been crucified with Christ; it is no longer I who live, but Christ lives in me; and the life which I now live in the flesh I live by faith in the Son of God, who loved me and gave Himself for me" *(Gal. 2:20)*.

Master Emotions

Ultimately, we must realize being self-controlled is God-controlled. Instead of allowing our emotions free reign, let us surrender to God. As women, we must be especially careful to control our emotions. Do you make decisions based only on feelings? Do you allow emotions like resentment, envy, bitterness, or anger to take root? Does your family know you are having a bad day the minute you enter the room? Do you fly off the handle when things don't go your way? Ask yourself, "How would my husband or children describe me?"

Remember, "A fool vents all his feelings, but a wise man holds them back" *(Prov. 29:11)*. "He who is slow to wrath has great understanding, but he who is impulsive exalts folly. A sound heart is life to the body, but envy is rottenness to the bones" *(Prov. 14:29-30)*.

Do you labor to make your home a peaceful dwelling, or is it a place that everyone can't wait to leave? "Better to dwell in the wilderness, than with a contentious and angry woman" *(Prov. 21:19)*

By failing to regulate our emotions, we can quickly damage our relationships with our husbands and children. Alternatively, we can nurture a beautiful atmosphere in our homes if we use our God-given emotions as He intended.

Create Good Habits

Appetites can be changed when we are motivated by a greater desire. As we draw closer to God, our eagerness to serve Him motivates change. Start small. Practicing control over little things will make it easier to rule over more significant areas of our lives.

Scientists have learned that the more decisions we have to make, the harder it is to maintain self-control. Sometimes this is described as decision fatigue. Also, stress and exhaustion lower our ability to maintain self-control. If we develop habits, patterns of behavior established by frequent repetition, we don't have to decide what we will or will not do. Often this is how bad habits start. Create good habits by being intentional.

For example, if you want to stop texting while driving *(which is an area in which one should develop self-control)*, create a habit of putting your phone in the glove box every time you get in the car. If you have difficulty getting to Sunday morning worship on time, set the alarm for Saturday night to remind yourself to get everything ready for the morning.

Research shows it takes at the very least three weeks to create new habits, but it may be more like 60 days, and for some people could take six months or more depending upon the habit that you are trying to establish. Don't give up. Habits that you cultivate today will help your self-control for years to come.

Address Your Weaknesses

We must be honest about our cravings, desires, and weaknesses. If we don't take responsibility and admit to ourselves what our struggles are, we will never conquer them. Once we recognize them, we can start cultivating self-control to overcome them.

Start with the tongue. "For we all stumble in many things. If anyone does not stumble in word, he is a perfect man, able also to bridle the whole body" *(Jas. 3:2)*. "In the multitude of words sin is not lacking, but he who restrains his lips is wise" *(Prov. 10:19)*. As women, we like to talk! But this can get us into trouble if we are not intentional with our words. Do I speak the truth? Are my words edifying? Do I gossip or brag? Do I speak harshly to others? Paul admonishes us as Christians to "let your speech always be with grace, seasoned with salt, that you may know how you ought to answer each one" *(Col. 4:6)*. Too often, the lack of control over our tongues impairs our relationship with our brothers and sisters in Christ. We must restrain our words if we hope to build up the body of Christ and represent Christ to the world.

Acknowledge the Possibility

God wouldn't call us to be self-controlled if it weren't possible. Yet, sometimes we need to acknowledge to ourselves that we have the strength to do it. Not too long ago, we were trying to eat healthier at our house, and the kids would often crave some kind of junk food that they did not need. To help them overcome their cravings, I began saying, "You are stronger than a bag of chips" or "you are stronger than a bowl of ice cream." And it worked! Since that time, the phrase has carried over into other aspects of our lives. Now, for example, when dealing with selfishness in a child, I will say, "God made you stronger than your desire for that toy." I have even discovered I say it to myself. Try it!

Look for the Way of Escape

When desires tempt us, God will provide a way of escape *(1 Cor 10:13)*. However, we must look for it. Sometimes that will mean planning ahead, knowing all of the if-then scenarios. "A prudent man foresees evil and hides himself, but the simple pass on and are punished" *(Prov. 22:3)*. It will also mean we need to say "No" as Joseph did when faced with sexual temptation *(Gen. 39:8)*. If the problem remains persistent, there may be times when we, like Joseph, are forced to flee *(Gen. 39:12)*. Remember Paul's exhortation to Timothy: "Flee also youthful lusts; but pursue righteousness, faith, love, peace with those who call on the Lord out of a pure heart. But avoid foolish and ignorant disputes, knowing that they generate strife" *(2 Tim 2:22-23)*.

Dangers are not always obvious. Are you tired because you have made too many commitments? Why do we try to do it all? We just hate to say no! Before we realize it, we can quickly become over-committed and overwhelmed. It isn't that we are squandering time in evil activities. Usually, we are involved in good things. However, when we stretch ourselves too thin, we can be so worn out that we neglect to spend time in prayer and studying God's word. This weakens our relationship with Him.

At the other end of the spectrum, we can be guilty of laziness and wasting our time. Have you ever lost track of time on social media sites and neglected your duties as a wife and mother? Paul said, "See then that you walk circumspectly, not as fools but as wise, redeeming the time, because the days are evil" *(Eph. 5:15-16)*. Mastering self results in making good use of our time.

Conclusion

For women professing to be led by the Spirit, the need for self-control extends to every aspect of our lives. It keeps us from sinning, motivates us to grow in righteousness, and helps us maintain a proper balance. Therefore, we must ask ourselves, is there any aspect of my life that is enslaved to my impulses, cravings, or desires? Do I have an appetite for something that I am trying to satisfy apart from God? Am I mastering myself in such a way that I can grow closer to God? Am I imbalanced in certain areas of life? If so, we need to bring those areas under His control. Are you led by God's Spirit or your own? Are you cultivating the peaceable fruit of righteousness *(Heb. 12:11)*. As Henry Liddon once said:

> What we do upon a great occasion will probably depend upon what we already are; what we are will be the result of previous years of self-discipline, under the grace of Christ or the absence of it *(Dictionary of Burning Words of Brilliant Writers, 2)*.

When Paul stood before Felix, attempting to explain what faith in Christ was all about, he reasoned with him about righteousness, self-control, and the judgment to come *(Acts 24:24-25)*. As disciples of Christ, we must be characterized as people who live righteously by practicing self-control because there will be a judgment. Let us look to Jesus, our ultimate example of ruling over oneself. In coming to earth, He willingly gave up the glories of heaven *(Phil. 2:3-8)*. When He was reviled, He did not revile in return *(1 Pet. 2:21-23)*. Facing the cross, He submitted to His Father— "not as I will, but as You will" *(Matt. 26:39)*. Let His example motivate us to be women characterized by self-control, displaying God's glory by His fruit in our lives.

Sources

BDAG = Arndt, William. et al. *A Greek-English Lexicon of the New Testament and Other Early Christian Literature.* Chicago: University of Chicago Press, 2000.

Duhigg, Charles. *The Power of Habit: Why We Do What We Do in Life and Business.* New York: Random House, 2012.

Henry, Gary. "Where Self-Discipline Comes From." *Reaching Forward: Daily Motivation to Move Ahead More Steadily.* Louisville, KY: WordPoints, 2009.

Himmel, Irvin. "Maturity." *Truth Magazine* 44.20 *(Oct. 17, 2020)*: 12.

Jordan, William George. *Self-Control: Its Kingship and Majesty.* Originally published 1905; Reprinted ed. Lexington, KY. 2018.

Liddon, Henry Parry. *Dictionary of Burning Words of Brilliant Writers.* Edited by Josiah Hotchkiss Gilbert. New York: Wilbur B. Ketcham, 1895. https://archive.org/details/dictionaryburni00gilbgoog/page/n6/mode/2up.

Merriam-Webster's Collegiate Dictionary. Springfield, MA: Merriam-Webster, 1996.

Mischel, Walter. *The Marshmallow Test: Mastering Self-Control.* New York: Little, Brown, and Co., 2014.

Thayer, Joseph Henry. *A Greek-English Lexicon of the New Testament.* New York: Harper & Brothers., 1889. Accessed via https://www.blueletterbible.org/.

Welch, Edward. "Self-Control: The Battle against 'One More.'" *The Journal of Biblical Counseling 19.2 (2001)*: 24-30.

Thought Questions

1. What are the benefits of living without self-control? What are the pitfalls of living without self-control?

2. Can you think of a "minor" area in your life in which you learned self-control? By what process did the change occur? How long did it take you to overcome? How did it change your daily life?

3. How can embedding the word of God in your heart produce self-control in your life? Please provide at least two verses to demonstrate this principle.

4. What is the strongest impediment to the development of self-control? Please provide at least two verses to explain how that impediment should be addressed.

5. How does self-control affect that feeling of "I just need to vent"? Please provide at least two verses to address the idea of emotional venting.

Concept Seeds

To begin preparation for the next lesson, please consider the following question:

Would the people who are around me say I create an atmosphere of blessing to them with my words?

The Fruit of Our Lips
By Diane Bain

Introduction

Proverbs 18:21 declares, "Death and Life are in the power of the tongue, and those who love it will eat its fruit." Thus, our words can do enormous good and enormous damage or evil. Our words can be life-giving or life-destroying. They have the power to kill and give life. Whether the words are thoughtless and careless, or expressions of thanksgiving and praise, fruit is born with every word. That's pretty incredible power. James echoes this theme: "So also the tongue is a small member, yet it boasts of great things" *(3:5)*. Yet, it is a small member, but the impact is enormous *(Prov. 15:1)*.

Speech is a gift of God, but He intends that our tongues be used for exhorting, encouraging, and upbuilding. Use the blessing of speech to edify and express wisdom. May our words be kind, true, and befitting.

Powerful Words

Words exhibit power, possessing the ability to wound or to heal. "There is one who speaks rashly like the thrusts of a sword, but the tongue of the wise brings healing" *(Prov. 12:18)*. Words carelessly spoken are sharp like swords. When blurted out in haste, perhaps under the pressure of the moment, our words may inflict significant damage, even though it was not our intention to do so. On the other hand, if we are wise with our words, we can minister grace, help, and health to the physical and spiritual condition of others as Proverbs 16:24 says,

"Pleasant words are like a honeycomb, sweetness to the soul and health to the bones."

Speaking of healing, Proverbs 12:25 indicates that good words can help cure depression. "Anxiety in a man's heart weighs it down, But a good word makes it glad." Have you ever been physically or spiritually low, then someone calls, or you pass somebody at worship services, or someone in the family just speaks a word of grace: "I know this is a hard time for you, but I have been praying for you, and I know you're going to make it."? Those soothing words promote health and wholeness in your spirit. Those are fruitful lips of kindness, truth, and blessing. What a joy it is to speak life-giving, healing words to another. They can be like a spring of cool water to a weary, thirsty traveler in the desert.

It is such a joy to be around people that offer nourishing words: words of encouragement and motivation. Some people are just naturally encouragers. We love their presence in our lives. As you think about these people in your life, who create an atmosphere and an attitude of blessing around you by the fruit of their lips, ask yourself: "Would the people who are around me say I create an atmosphere of blessing to them with my words?" Ask God to help you be that person.

Fruitful Words of a Mother

A child's heart is like wet cement; the impressions created early in life harden over time. Your child's identity, capability, and self-worth depend primarily upon the words you speak to them as they grow in your care.

Your mouth, as a mother, can offer a great blessing to your children. In instruction and correction, let your words be full of love, encouragement, positive reinforcement, blessing, grace, and kindness. You can speak words that nurture and heal and strengthen insecure teenagers.

By the same token, those thoughtless words spoken in the heat of the moment can do enormous damage. Ponder the homes that have been torn apart, and children that have been devastated—because the wife or mother did not control her tongue.

Fruitful Words of a Wife

To a husband, the words of a wife bring life or death. Our words bring hope and encouragement, or doubt and discouragement. Our words build him up or tear him down. Words are never neutral. They have an influence, for good or bad. Showing respect and admiration through your words draws your husband closer to you. We may think praise and admiration seem to be little things, but they can make a big difference.

What a different mood that wives create when we take a few minutes to express love and concern. How long does it take to smile, or hug, or say, "How was your day?" With conscious effort, we pleasantly greet people throughout the day, but many times we fail to carry that same attitude home with us.

Do you want to encourage your husband? First, show appreciation for what he does for you. Second, encourage him in his work as well as other endeavors by complimenting him for a job well done. Third, remember to say, and often say, "I love you."

A survey followed 300 couples for twenty-two years. Among the happiest couples, a profound thing stood out: Wives who regularly affirmed their husbands made a significant positive impact on their marriage. Such words are the fruit of our lips.

30-Day Husband Challenge for a Wife

Ladies, if you struggle with speaking kind words to your husband, take the "30-day Husband Challenge for a Wife." Here it is: For the next thirty days, you cannot say anything negative about your husband, either to him or anyone else. Instead, express something you admire or appreciate about your husband, to him, and to someone else. You will see amazing things happen to you, your husband, and your marriage. You will love the fruit this simple challenge bears!

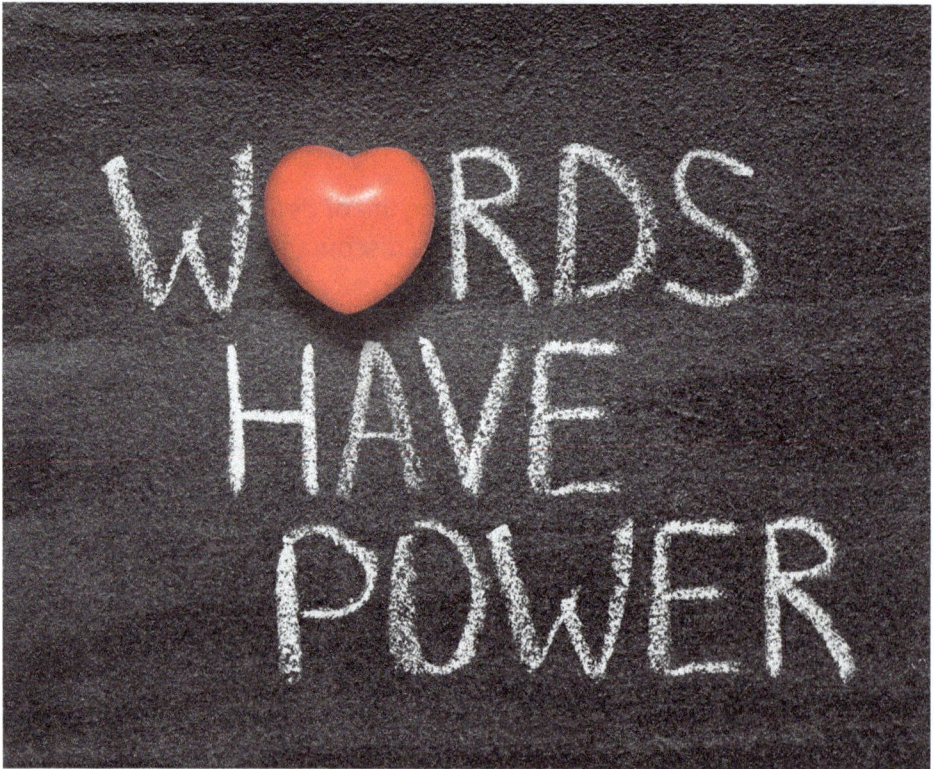

By Their Words, You Will Know Their Heart

In Luke 6:45, Jesus affirmed, "The good man out of the good treasure of his heart brings forth what is good, and the evil man out of the evil treasure brings forth what is evil; for his mouth speaks from that which fills his heart." Your tongue reveals the condition of your heart. Your words are a mirror into your heart.

Consider each kind of heart, and think of the words that emerge from it:

Heart Condition	Resulting Speech
Critical Heart	
Mean-spirited heart	
Proud heart	
Angry heart	
Discontented heart	
Evil heart	

Conversely, a *pure and righteous heart* will overflow with pure and righteous words. A *loving heart* speaks love. A *kind heart* speaks kindness. A *humble heart* speaks humility and submission. Pure, loving, kind, humble hearts do not seek to draw attention to oneself or one's accomplishments. Instead, they have a way of lifting others up with edifying words *(Eph. 4:29)*. Such a heart will have the attitude of John the Baptist, who spoke of Jesus, "He must increase, and I must decrease" *(John 3:30)*.

If you have a heart for God, a spiritually-minded heart, your speech communicates spiritual truths and offers praise to God, leading others to understand the awe and amazement of God. Scripture says, "Through Jesus, let us continually offer up a sacrifice of praise to God, that is, the fruit of our lips that gave thanks to His name" *(Heb. 13:15)*.

The Proper Source of Fruitful Words

A heart filled with the word of God produces the righteous fruit from our lips. Proverbs 30:5 says, "Every word of God is pure." If your mind and heart are filled with the word of God, then as you are pushed, shoved, or squeezed by life's circumstances, what is going to come out? Should it not be pure words—the word of God?

Proverbs 2:6 tells us, "The Lord gives wisdom." Only a wise heart speaks wise words. Where do you receive such wisdom? "From His mouth come knowledge and understanding." Such wisdom cannot be found listening to worldly ideas, philosophies, and beliefs. Letting your heart feed upon the message of the culture will fill your heart with words that will cause you to talk like the world. Nevertheless, the book of Proverbs contains numerous examples of the need for a heart of wisdom that comes from God to speak words of knowledge and understanding.

The worthy woman of Proverbs 31 is an outstanding example of wisdom. I am encouraged and challenged to be this woman. She is a woman of virtue. The Bible says, "She opens her mouth with wisdom and on her tongue is the law of kindness" *(Prov. 31:26)*. Would your family say this verse describes you? Whether she is giving direction or instruction to her children or providing her family with the law, her words are still filled with kindness. She is the wise and kind woman that I want to be.

Fruitful words come from a choice we make to bring "every thought captive to obey Christ" *(2 Cor. 10:5)*. Such a desire requires conscious, disciplined effort and time spent at the feet of Jesus, fixing our eyes on Him. Meditating daily upon His words, we are transformed by the renewal of our minds *(Rom. 12:2)*. This is why we should get up early in the morning and get into the word of God. May it saturate our minds and our hearts. May it cleanse us, wash us, and fill us, so by God's grace, the words we speak today will be words of wisdom.

We would do well to make the psalmist's prayer our own: "Let the words of my mouth and the meditation of my heart be acceptable in your sight, O Lord, my rock and my redeemer" *(Ps. 19:14)*. For this to

be true, a guard needs to be placed upon the mouth. Ask God to be your guard for your heart and tongue. Scripture says if you guard your mouth, invoking the Lord's help, He will keep your soul from destruction and trouble. "He who guards his mouth preserves life, but he who opens wide his lips shall have destruction" *(Prov. 13:3)*. "Whoever guards his mouth and tongue keeps his soul from troubles" *(Prov. 21:23)*. "Set a guard, O Lord, over my mouth; Keep watch over the door of my lips" *(Ps. 141:3)*. A wise woman will ask God to keep watch over her words.

Conclusion

How you speak and what you say matters to God. Whether in your marriage, family, church, or workplace. Each day presents opportunities to speak angry, sarcastic, belittling, or gossiping words. Yet, it also offers opportunities to speak words of blessing, praise, and encouragement to others.

May God help us use our tongues to build up those around us rather than tearing them down. Above all, let us speak words to honor Christ, adorning His gospel, and displaying His loveliness. Speak words worthy of women whose hearts have been won by His amazing grace.

Thought Questions

1. Can you think of an example in your life where someone's words powerfully affected you, encouraged you, or even devastated you?

2. Can you finish this sentence with three ideas? Because words contain power, I will _____, _____, and _____.

3. In your opinion, why do the effects of a mother's words last throughout a person's lifetime?

4. How should this realization change your interactions with the children?

5. In your opinion, why do the wife's words have the power to make or break her man?

6. What are your two favorite verses from Proverbs discussed in this lesson? Please explain why.

7. What does James say about the power of the tongue *(cf. Jas. 3)*.

Concept Seeds

To begin preparation for the next lesson, please consider the following questions:

For what purposes did God create you? Are you fulfilling those purposes in your life?

The Withered Fig Tree: Anti-Fruit
By Elizabeth Cazan

Introduction

Seeing a lone fig tree by the road, He came to it and found nothing on it except leaves only; and He said to it, "No longer shall there ever be any fruit from you." And at once, the fig tree withered (Matt. 21:19).

Until a few months ago, my only experience with figs was through cookies. This opportunity to take a more in-depth look at the withered fig opened my eyes to three valuable spiritual lessons. First, God created all things, including us, for a purpose. He also expects fruitfulness from His creation, including us. Finally, Jesus is the perfect Judge of the fig tree, and also of us.

Purpose

All creation glorifies God. How does a plant or an animal *(such as a tree or an ostrich)* offer praise to God? It does so by doing what it was created to do. When God answered Job from the whirlwind, describing one of His more unique creations, He observed:

The ostriches' wings flap joyously with the pinion and plumage of love, for she abandons her eggs to the earth and warms them in the dust, and she forgets that a foot may crush them, or that a wild beast may trample them. She treats her young cruelly, as if they were not hers; though her labor be in vain, she is unconcerned; because God has made her forget wisdom, and has not given her a share of understanding. When she lifts herself on high, she laughs at the horse and his rider (Job 39:13-18).

God made the ostrich the way that she is. He does not expect the ostrich to be a noble, intelligent bird. Instead, she brings glory to God by being what she was created to be. In the same manner, a tree glorifies God in being what it was created to be a tree. If a tree tried to be something that it was not intended to be, it would dishonor God instead of glorifying Him. All creation glorifies God by fulfilling its intended purpose.

In creating the world and all that is in it, God made it with a purpose in mind. In Isaiah 43:1-7, God identifies His reasons for bringing forth Israel as a nation: "Because you are precious in My eyes and honored, and I love you." He then issues a general call to "everyone who is called by My name, whom I created for My glory, whom I formed and made."

We *can* know exactly why God created us: for His glory because He is worthy. The apostle John proclaims, "Worthy are You, our Lord and our God, to receive glory and honor and power; for You created all things, and because of Your will they existed and were created" (Rev. 4:11). Paul said, "Whatever you do, do all to the glory of God" (1 Cor. 10:31). Jesus said, "Let your light shine before others, so that they may see your good works and give glory to your Father, who is in heaven" (Matt. 5:16).

Solomon summarizes God's design for His people: "Fear God and keep His commandments for this is the whole duty of man" (Eccl. 12:13-14). That's our purpose. We exist to bring glory to God, just like all of creation.

The fig tree was cursed by Jesus because it was not fulfilling its purpose as a fig tree. It proved useless to God, just when it was needed. In the parable of the vinedresser in Luke 13:6-9, the landowner came expecting fruit and found none. He told the vinedresser to cut it down and not waste the land with it. Contextually, Jesus was calling the people to repent lest they perish. We must bear fruit while there is time and opportunity. To remain unfruitful is to risk destruction.

And He began telling this parable: "A man had a fig tree which had been planted in his vineyard; and he came looking for fruit on it and did not find any. And he said to the vineyard-keeper, 'Behold, for three years I have come looking for fruit on this fig tree without finding any. Cut it down! Why does it even use up the ground?' And he answered and said to him, 'Let it alone, sir, for this year too, until I dig around it and put in fertilizer; and if it bears fruit next year, fine; but if not, cut it down'" (Luke 13:6-9).

Once, I had a little orange tree that I potted and tended. I put it in my kitchen and dreamed of its fragrant blossoms filling the house with a pleasant, citrus aroma. I waited years and got absolutely nothing—not even one flower. I potted and repotted it and tried various plant foods and soils, but without effect. So, I pulled it out by the roots and threw it out into the ditch. We see this every day in our lives. However, do we recognize the parallel in our spiritual lives? Our purpose is to glorify God. Jesus tells us we glorify the Father by bearing much fruit *(John 15:8)*. The only way to do this is by being in Jesus Christ, the True Vine *(John 15:5)*. Are you fruitful?

God Expects Fruitfulness

Just as a healthy tree manifests itself by producing fruit, Christians also manifest healthy spiritual lives by producing fruit. Peter offers tools for success: "Add to your faith virtue; and to virtue knowledge; And to knowledge temperance; and to temperance patience; and to patience godliness; And to godliness brotherly kindness; and to brotherly kindness charity. For if these things be in you, and abound, they make you that ye shall neither be barren nor unfruitful in the knowledge of our Lord Jesus Christ" *(2 Pet. 1: 5-8)*.

Just as Jesus expected there to be fruit on the fig tree, He also expects there to be fruit present in our lives. There is no such thing as an "unfruitful Christian." All Christians produce fruit to varying degrees, but unfruitful Christians will be cut off and cast into the fire. John 15:2 states, "Every branch *in Me* that does not bear fruit he takes away, and every branch that does bear fruit he prunes, that it may bear more fruit" *(emphasis mine)*. God expects fruitfulness. Disciples have varying degrees of abilities and achieve differing results; nevertheless, fruitfulness is required of all.

The first mention of the fig tree was in the garden of Eden when Adam and Eve sewed fig leaves together to cover their nakedness *(Gen. 3:7)*. Eve used the fig tree for an unintended purpose, but at least it was useful for something. Jesus came to the fig tree to use it for its intended purpose. The Creator planned to use the fruit from the tree for Himself. He was hungry and expected fruit on the tree, but there was nothing. Likewise, when God looks at your life, does He see the fruit that He can use for Himself and His purposes? Colossians 1:10 encourages us to walk in a "manner worthy of the Lord, fully pleasing to Him, bearing fruit in every good work and increasing in the knowledge of God." Are you outwardly hardy and green but spiritually fruitless? When the Creator needs to use you in His service, will you be ready?

Jesus as Judge

When Jesus found no fruit on the fig tree, He cursed it so that it withered to the roots. This miracle stands out from others in that it was one of destruction and not one of restoration. We may wonder, why didn't Jesus choose to rejuvenate the plant so that it would produce fruit? In this encounter, we see Jesus as Judge.

We first learn of Jesus as Judge from John the Baptist. Speaking of the One who was coming, John said, "His winnowing fork is in His hand, and He will clear His threshing floor and gather His wheat into the barn, but the chaff He will burn with unquenchable fire" *(Matt. 3:12)*. Having lived a flawless life, God has given Him all authority as Judge *(John 5:22)*. Jesus possesses full jurisdiction over life and death. Just as He proclaimed death to the unfruitful fig tree, He will also proclaim our end. "For we must all appear before the judgment seat of Christ, so that each one may receive what is due for what he has done in the body, whether good or evil" *(2 Cor 5:10)*.

We might ask, "*Why* did Jesus curse the tree?" His disciples, who were present, wondered *how* this happened. Even in the last week before His betrayal, they were still struggling to comprehend His power. Accordingly, Jesus, their Savior, encourages them to grow in their faith:

Seeing this, the disciples were amazed and asked, "How did the fig tree wither all at once?" And Jesus answered and said to them, "Truly I say to you, if you have faith and do not doubt, you will not only do what was done to the fig tree, but even if you say to this mountain, 'Be taken up and cast into the sea,' it will happen. And all things you ask in prayer, believing, you will receive" *(Matt. 21:20-22)*.

Conclusion

The miracle of the withered fig tree stumps many of us today. Examining this story, we learn several valuable spiritual lessons that increase our understanding of this miracle: God created us with a purpose. God expects fruitfulness in Christians. Finally, Jesus is the perfect Judge.

Thought Questions

1. Think of your favorite flower. How does the flower bring glory to God?

2. As you examine it, what do you learn about the One who created it?

3. Can you think of two Bible examples in which the natural creation displays or magnifies God's glory? Please list your verses.

4. Can you offer specific examples from your own life when you noticed the Spirit's fruit?

5. At times when a Christian is not displaying the Spirit's fruit, what is the problem? What passages of Scripture support your answer?

6. What does Jesus's judgment of the fig tree teach you about Him?

7. What did He say about the necessity of bearing fruit *(John 15:1-8)*.

Concept Seeds

To begin preparation for the next lesson, please consider the following question:

In what ways will bearing the fruit of the Spirit impact my family?

The Fruitful Family
By Alena Brown

Introduction

"Family" is always a timely topic. The home was God's first institution and covenant with mankind. God cemented Adam and Eve, the first man and woman, together, beginning the first family. Satan targets the home because of its effectiveness in glorifying God and spreading the gospel. Because of the institution of the family, humans can create more worshippers, ultimately multiplying the number of those bowing down to our Lord in praise and adoration.

In our homes and families, the fruit of the Spirit identifies households that are being led by the Spirit. It is evidence of a vigorous plant with deep, steadfast roots, enabling us to stand against the storms and trials of this life. A family that possesses the fruit of the Spirit is not limited in its effectiveness of shining Christ's light to all who see it. People will take notice, watching in wonder at the joy and contentment shown by the fruitful family. Hopefully, they will also ponder the source of such grace and goodness. Non-Christians might open their hearts to a purpose beyond self and indeed search for our Lord. Fellow Christians rejoice that other godly families exemplify a testimony to God's creation and perfect design. It brings a smile to our faces and joy to our hearts to see a loving couple bring up more lovers of the word and future workers in the kingdom.

The Fruitful Wife

As wives, let us consider our marriages. How does possessing the fruit of the Spirit serve to bless our homes? A husband cannot do all he is called to do without his wife's *love*, *joy*, and *patience*. Our efforts to be *peaceful* during a disagreement can allow for a speedy, peaceful resolution. Our *kindness* to listen to the events of a rough day at the office can bring him mental clarity and relaxation. Our *goodness* and *faithfulness* to run his home and anticipate his needs make us more precious to him than rubies. Our *gentleness* can bring a smile to his face and place a song in his heart. When we disagree with a decision that our husband has made, practicing *self-control* will ensure that he has our support and will show appreciation for tough decisions.

Proverbs 31:11-12 says, "The heart of her husband safely trusts her; so he will have no lack of gain. She does him good and not evil all the days of her life." Your husband has entrusted you to run his home in a godly manner. Your efforts to create a peaceful home and do good will allow him to focus on the task of leadership God has given him and will give him the strength to do so, knowing he has you as his helper. He will be confident that your advice is godly and Spirit-led because God's fruits are evident in your life. The weight your husband carries as the home's spiritual leader necessitates your prayerful thoughtfulness and evident appreciation for his task at hand. He will make mistakes, but it is better for him to lead poorly than for you to lead the home well. Being submissive to him will keep the sweet unity God intended and not allow the devil to put his foot in the door of your marriage. Endeavor to keep your marital bond a sacred, God-glorifying union.

Hear the sweet anticipation a godly man can have in Psalm 128:3: "Your wife shall be like a fruitful vine in the very heart of your house." Considering the context of Psalm 128, the author is stating that one of the blessings a godly man can have is a fruitful wife in the sense of bearing children for him. However, productivity beyond that of bearing children could also be applied. Busily working in the home to keep the necessary elements of physical life going is a blessing to your husband.

Caring for the children, providing delicious, healthy meals, and being thrifty with money will ensure your husband's trust for you to make wise household decisions *(Prov. 31:13-18, 27, 31)*. Much of the joy and peace in the home centers around the wife and mother because she seems to hold in her possession "the very heart of the house."

The Blessing of Children

And what about those sweet, precious children? What about those little olive plants that come ready to permanently take on the imprint of the hand from which they are being molded? Molding souls is a delicate task and will only be done effectively after giving oneself over to be a vessel for the Lord's work. The psalmist compares children in Psalm 128:3 to that of olive plants all around the dinner table, bringing the God-fearing man joy and happiness. The product of a loving home that possesses the fruit of the Spirit will be one of contentment and delight as their family expands.

Psalm 127:3 says, "Behold, children are a heritage from the Lord, the fruit of the womb is a reward. Like arrows in the hand of a warrior, so are the children of one's youth. Happy is the man who has his quiver full of *them*. . ." Praise the Lord for children! Nothing else in this physical creation provides a clearer insight into our relationship with our heavenly Father than having children ourselves.

Here they are pictured as arrows in the hand of a warrior. Why would God give us little arrows? For what are they used? What battle are we in where weaponry would be useful? It is for a spiritual battle going on in the "heavenlies" that our children are so desperately needed *(Eph. 6:12)*. The fathers are pictured in Psalm 127 as warriors. They are strong fighters against evil and Satan. They are leaders and defenders of truth. Children can serve to further the gospel, reaching places the parents could not reach alone. God uses young families while little ones are still being trained to be an example to the world, and He will then use those trained soldiers when they are adults as they enlist in His army. It is God's beautiful design that fathers raise and train children for His glory,

ready to be shot out as arrows into this dark world to be workers in His kingdom and combat evil. They must continue to fight for truth and for lost souls.

Verse 3 of Psalm 127 also refers to children as "a reward" for the godly man. To think of them as a reward, we must have the proper view of children. The psalmist calls them a blessing or gift from the Creator Himself. They come full of energy, purity, and endless potential. Do we have the proper view of children? Are they inconvenient? Do they cramp our lifestyle? Or do we see them as a heritage—a way to pass on to future generations the most important name and inheritance they could be given? Do we recognize them as a way for the gospel to keep spreading and workers to be multiplied?

In Psalms 127 and 128, the inspired writer poetically shares the secret of a happy home. Solomon offers a warning: "Unless the Lord builds the house, they labor in vain who build it; Unless the Lord guards the city, The watchman stays awake in vain" *(127:1)* Our families are constantly under attack, in dire jeopardy of being torn apart by divorce, rebellion, apathy, or a disregard of God's pattern for building it. We must protect our homes from the evil one. It is God who designed marriage and family, and unless He is building the essence of our homes, and unless He creates its fortress and is its guard, all human efforts are sure to be in vain.

Verse 2 continues: "It is vain for you to rise up early, to sit up late, to eat the bread of sorrows. . . ." No matter what else we do, nothing is as important as God's word being implemented in the home. To make our families the best and most effective they can be, we need to follow His perfect blueprint. There is not much outside the four walls of our homes that we control. Inside this sacred area, we strive to create a holy, God-glorifying place where His presence can be felt.

The Fruitful Mother

One cannot underestimate the power of the fruit of the Spirit in raising our children. If children have our unconditional *love* they will feel it. Our *joy* and *peace* result in happiness and contentment because Mama is showing it lived out. Our *patience* will allow for milk being spilled and jelly to be on the carpet without anger for simple clumsiness and childhood mistakes. Our *kindness* for "boo-boos" and "owies" will breed tenderness and compassion for others within them. *Goodness* shown as a mother is hospitable to others or takes food to the homeless shelter with her children at her side shows them true servanthood. Our *faithfulness* for the task at hand will bring them the security that Mama will always be there and is faithful to God and her husband no matter what life throws at us. It is *gentleness* that calms their spirits and gives them certainty about our intentions toward their wellbeing. And it is *self-control* that allows discipline and training to be effective, often despite the ache in our hearts to carry it out and see it through.

Maintaining the fruit of the Spirit in our lives and applying these concepts when raising our children ensures their ability to see Christ living in our hearts. It allows proper discernment and clarity for the Spirit's guidance while disciplining and training them. It also gives our children a beautiful picture of God's love and consistency as they grow and become His, and there is a necessary transfer of accountability from the parent to our Lord.

The Spiritual Home

Isn't it interesting that often, the core of who we are is revealed within the home? Here we find ourselves looking in a mirror and seeing the deficiencies of our hearts. It might be somewhat easy to refine ourselves publicly at worship services and in the community. We polish our appearance, manifest good attitudes, and give our best to love and serve others. We have all good intentions of living with others in a holy, Christ-like way before the Lord. Our efforts are commendable, but somehow when we enter the walls of familiarity with the people closest to us, the purposeful straining of efforts stops. Suddenly, at our core, we are not as polished and Christ-like as we might have thought. That is where some works of the flesh might be revealed: hatred, jealousies, outbursts of anger, and selfish ambitions. It is among our family that we realize if the "fruit" from our "tree" actually belongs to the Spirit, then it bears and produces *all* the time.

Honest, prayerful searching helps humbly discern whether any of these descriptions of the works of the flesh could describe us. Part of dying to self and living for Christ is recognizing sin and putting it away *(Eph. 4:17-24)*. Allowing ourselves to be filled with the Spirit and used as His temple will mean He has complete control of every thought, every word, and every decision *(2 Cor. 10:5; Rom. 8:5-11)*. Every nook and cranny of our hearts should be filled with God's love, goodness, and holiness. His fruit will begin to bear, and we will look more and more like Jesus. Such "holy living" will bleed into our homes, allowing the presence of the Lord to be felt there. In turn, this creates a powerful weapon against Satan and a powerful testimony for God's grace.

God entrusted us, women, with special charge—that of running and managing the home *(Titus 2:5)*. Our particular jurisdiction is in which serving our husbands and raising our children. This holds the highest priority. Clothing ourselves in the fruit of the Spirit is paramount to doing our best to serve the Lord within the realm of the responsibilities given to us. Possessing the fruit of the Spirit will demonstrate whether or not Christ truly reigns in our hearts as King, as we seek to be productive homemakers for Him.

Conclusion

There is hardly a better example of the closeness of Christ and the church than the beauty, love, and intimacy that occurs in the one-flesh relationship. No better pattern is there of our relationship with our heavenly Father than little ones being born and raised as a result of this union. Many spiritual lessons and understandings are rooted in the sweetness of this earthly relationship that can aid our spiritual growth and understanding. Cultivating the fruit of the Spirit in our homes, refining and polishing these essential qualities, helps us to point the world to Jesus more effectively. The family remains one of God's most important strongholds for steadfastness and growth within the Lord's kingdom. The effectiveness of the family as a godly example in reaching the lost is unsurpassed. Let's embrace this tool and be fruitful and productive for His glory as the Spirit reigns in us.

Sources

Arndt, William et al. *A Greek-English Lexicon of the New Testament and Other Early Christian Literature.* Chicago: University of Chicago Press, 2000.

Thought Questions

1. In what ways does the fruit of the Spirit positively identify God-centered families?

2. In your opinion, what are three home-based activities that nourish active spiritual growth?

3. In your opinion, what are three home-based activities that subvert spiritual growth?

4. Why do you think it is challenging to display the fruit of the Spirit with members of our families?

5. In what ways can a Spirit-led family magnify God's wisdom?

6. How is modern, militant feminism an assault upon God's pattern for the home?

7. Contrast the fruit of feminism with benefits of embracing the biblical pattern for the home, the male/female relationships, parenting and personal fulfillment.

Concept Seeds

Having studied these essays on the Spirit's Fruit, please consider the following questions:

What have I earned in these studies that I had not considered before? How can I better apply these things to my life?

www.ingramcontent.com/pod-product-compliance
Lightning Source LLC
Chambersburg PA
CBHW051425090426
42737CB00014B/2837